# CONTENTS

KT-873-112

# PART FOUR
## CRITICAL HISTORY

# PART FIVE
## BACKGROUND

# PART ONE

## INTRODUCTION

# HOW TO STUDY A NOVEL

Studying a novel on your own requires self-discipline and a carefully thought-out work plan in order to be effective.

- You will need to read the novel more than once. Start by reading it quickly for pleasure, then read it slowly and thoroughly.

- On your second reading make detailed notes on the plot, characters and themes of the novel. Further readings will generate new ideas and help you to memorise the details of the story.

- Some of the characters will develop as the plot unfolds. How do your responses towards them change during the course of the novel?

- Think about how the novel is narrated. From whose point of view are events described?

- A novel may or may not present events chronologically: the time-scheme may be a key to its structure and organisation.

- What part do the settings play in the novel?

- Are words, images or incidents repeated so as to give the work a pattern? Do such patterns help you to understand the novel's themes?

- Identify what styles of language are used in the novel.

- What is the effect of the novel's ending? Is the action completed and closed, or left incomplete and open?

- Does the novel present a moral and just world?

- Cite exact sources for all quotations, whether from the text itself or from critical commentaries. Wherever possible find your own examples from the novel to back up your opinions.

- Always express your ideas in your own words.

These York Notes offer an introduction to *Jane Eyre* and cannot substitute for close reading of the text and the study of secondary sources.

 **QUESTION**

Compare and contrast the role of narrator and 'Reader' in *Jane Eyre*.

 **QUESTION**

How is Rochester's character revealed?

# READING *JANE EYRE: AN AUTOBIOGRAPHY*

It is easy to identify with *Jane Eyre,* for though the novel was written over a century and a half ago Jane expresses a young girl's longing for fulfilment, and fulfilment on her own terms – a concept very much at odds with the dictates of society in her own day. "Wicked and cruel boy!" (Ch. 1, p. 17) she shouts at Master Reed in the first chapter, "You are like a murderer – you are like a slave-driver – you are like the Roman emperors!" And, "[d]id ever anybody see such a picture of passion!" (Ch. 1, p. 18) her witnesses declare. Jane's fierce rebellion is a constant throughout the book, and though she appears to follow customary practice, she actually grows to maturity as a sensible and strong-willed woman whose aspirations confound convention.

*Jane Eyre* is full of dramatic contrasts, in which the ordinary and everyday are set against the gothic, and is so packed with supernatural detail, coincidence and magic that it seems to be a fairytale even though it is built upon the foundations of everyday life. The narrative is forceful, vivid, and leaves a lasting impression of both anguish and delight. It is, however, carefully structured, controlled and coherent. It shows us how Brontë sought to write not only about what she observed, but also what was hidden and unseen. The form has been dictated by the theme and that theme is deeply felt.

As soon as *Jane Eyre* was published it became immensely popular, though it also attracted vehement criticism. This criticism emerged because of its attack on Evangelicalism and, given its quite explicit portrayal of physical and emotional desires, because of its supposedly coarse morality. With hindsight, the Victorian assessment can seem harsh, for though Jane is in part an advocate for her sex, she also has to combine passion with duty before she can live happily ever after. However, the values of our day differ considerably from those of Charlotte Brontë's.

The novel does not have a moral as such, Charlotte Brontë always resisted writing for a purpose. Rather it consists of a deep psychological insight into an individual's emotional and intellectual needs.

On one level, *Jane Eyre* is a romance, the story of two people falling in love and defying convention to be together. But this is also a story of a story of self-discovery. As we follow Jane, she grows and learns about the world around her – and learns more than mere books or schooling could teach her. In the process we experience her sincerity, her powerful feelings for Rochester and the intensity of their relationship. We see that ultimately Jane chooses Rochester over St John, because Jane comes to know herself and learns that the conventions of her day are simple habits of thought, not moral certainties. The sympathy that grows between Jane and Rochester is therefore much more than 'love', it is a sympathy of 'fellow-feeling; mutual sensibility; the quality of being affected by the affections [feelings] of another' as defined by Samuel Johnson in his *Dictionary* of 1755. In this respect Brontë was influenced by the school of emotional moral philosophy, whose followers believed that the emotions – or feeling as experienced through the sympathetic imagination – are meant to give us an innate sense of morality or to show us how our actions affect others.

**CHECK THE BOOK**

For a consideration of the gendered aspects of the way in which *Jane Eyre* was originally reviewed see N. D. Thompson *Reviewing Sex gender and the reception of Victorian novels* (1996).

**CHECK THE BOOK**

For an important nineteenth-century assessment of Charlotte Brontë's life and re-assessment of her work see Mrs Gaskell's *The Life of Charlotte Brontë* (1857).

# PART TWO

# THE TEXT

## NOTE ON THE TEXT

Begun in 1846, *Jane Eyre* was initially published in October 1847 by Smith, Elder & Co. in three volumes under the supposed editorship of 'Currer Bell'. The novel was so popular that a second edition appeared in January 1848, followed by a third in April of the same year. Brontë's publishers wanted her to illustrate the third edition, but she refused because she felt that she lacked the necessary skill. Also, she did not believe that her characters ought to have portraits because they were, 'mostly unattractive in looks'. The final version to be published during Charlotte Brontë's lifetime was a one-volume edition in 1850.

In each edition, except the last, corrections and small revisions were made by the author; however, each new edition also saw the introduction of new errors and misprints. More recent editors have often taken the liberty of correcting the text, especially in matters of spelling, punctuation and apparently accidental departures from earlier editions. The third edition sanctioned by Brontë therefore now forms the basis of most modern imprints of the novel, but many editors also refer to the manuscript used by the printers to set the first edition.

Unfortunately, the earlier Penguin Classics edition of 1966, reprinted in 1985, is now out of print, but is worth trying to get hold of as Q.D. Leavis' introduction and notes still provide the reader with some of the most thoughtful and thorough commentary available. One of the most useful modern editions is the Penguin Classics edition of 1996 edited, with introduction and notes by, Michael Mason; the text of this edition has been used in compiling this Note.

 **CHECK THE NET**

You can find a reliable e-text of *Jane Eyre* via Project Gutenberg at **http://www. gutenberg. net** — search for 'Brontë' under Author and 'Jane Eyre' under Title Word(s).

# SYNOPSIS

At the beginning of the novel Jane Eyre is an orphan who lives with her well-to-do aunt, Mrs Reed, and cousins, Eliza, John and Georgiana. Jane is constantly bullied by her cousins, and her aunt always assumes that she is the guilty party whenever there is a fight. On one occasion Mrs Reed locks Jane in a room that is reputedly haunted, as punishment for a crime that she did not commit. Jane's nerves are shattered and the servants' apothecary is called in. Immeasurably unhappy, Jane is deeply relieved to discover that he has recommended she be sent away to boarding school. Before she leaves she makes friends with Bessie, the nursemaid who 'had a remarkable knack of narrative' (Vol. I, Ch. 4, p. 38), and wins a psychological battle against her aunt.

Jane is then sent to Lowood, a school for clergymen's daughters, where she makes friends with another pupil, Helen Burns, and the mistress, Miss Temple. Helen, who is deeply religious, gentle and forbearing, teaches Jane the value of self-control. However, the conditions at the school are appalling and, when the girls become sick, Helen dies of consumption. As a result, the school is reformed and in the end Jane stays on for a total of eight years, as pupil, then as assistant teacher. When Miss Temple leaves to marry, Jane begins to find life at the school restrictive and advertises for a new job.

Jane is soon offered a place by a Mrs Fairfax as governess to 'a little girl, under ten years of age' (Vol. I, Ch. 10, pp. 102–3) at double her Lowood salary, and sets out to take up her new position as quickly as she can. When she arrives at Thornfield Hall she finds that Mrs Fairfax is housekeeper to the master, Edward Fairfax Rochester, and that the little girl, Adèle Varens, is his ward. The place suits Jane and she settles in quickly, but for some time does not see Rochester. She finally meets him as he rides towards Thornfield when she is out on an errand one day. His horse slips on some ice and he is obliged to seek her aid.

As they become better acquainted Jane begins to feel drawn to Rochester; he is equally attracted by her intelligence and wit. While

 **CHECK THE BOOK**

For a thorough history of the economic, social and ideological context in which *Jane Eyre* was written see L. Davidoff and C. Hall *Family Fortunes Men and Women of the English Middle Class 1780–1850* (2002).

**CONTEXT**

Divorce was rare at this point. Even after the Matrimonial Causes Act of 1857 a husband could divorce his wife for adultery, but a wife had to prove aggravation by cruelty or desertion.

**CONTEXT**

The school is a charitable establishment. Charity was an important part of Victorian life, it is estimated that Queen Victoria herself spent 10% of her income annually on good causes.

**CONTEXT**

Men ran Victorian India, but officials', not only missionaries', wives would often tour with their husbands and undertake local charitable and missionary work.

she is away from the hall visiting her dying aunt she misses him and he tries to make her jealous by pretending that he is going to marry a local heiress, Miss Blanche Ingram. In the end, despite the differences in their station and age, Rochester finally proposes and Jane accepts. The match is ill-omened, however, and their wedding is interrupted by the arrival of Mr Richard Mason who declares that Rochester is already married to his sister, Bertha Mason. It becomes clear that there is indeed a Mrs Rochester, but that she is a mad-woman, kept under lock and key in the attic of Thornfield. Rochester pleads for Jane to go abroad with him as his mistress, to become 'Mrs Rochester – both virtually and nominally' (Vol. III, Ch. 1, p. 342), but she cannot bring herself to stay and slips away from the hall before anyone can stop her.

Jane wanders destitute for some days. No-one will help her or give her work until she is finally taken in by a clergyman, St John Rivers, and his sisters, Diana and Mary, who find Jane half-starved at their door. As she recovers from her ordeal she makes friends with the sisters and St John offers her a job as the village schoolmistress. She works at the school under the assumed name of Jane Elliott, but St John discovers her real name on one of her drawings. Through this he is able to tell her that she is related to him and his sisters and that she has inherited a fortune from her uncle. She insists on sharing the money equally with her new-found family and hopes to be treated as their sister.

St John is a cold ambitious man, patient, forbearing, and exacting who hopes to become a missionary and, in the end, he asks Jane to marry him and travel to India as his help-mate. Jane says that though she might help him in his missionary work she cannot marry him because he does not love her. As he presses her on the matter and she begins to give way, she hears Rochester calling to her. Jane decides that she must find out what has become of Rochester before she can do anything else and travels back to Thornfield.

When she reaches Thornfield Jane discovers that the house has been razed to the ground and further investigation reveals that the hall has been burnt down by Mrs Rochester. Edward Rochester is alive, but, in the process of trying to save his wife, has suffered terrible injuries. Jane determines to find him and, though he is maimed and blind, they finally marry. The novel closes with an account of their married life and a brief summary of what has happened to Diana, Mary and St John Rivers.

## DETAILED SUMMARIES

# VOLUME I

### CHAPTER 1

- Jane flies at Master John.

**GLOSSARY**

*Bewick's History of British Birds* (1804) includes the quotations used (introduction of Volume II, p. xii) and many detailed vignettes

**Where ... Hebrides** from James Thomson, *The Seasons* (1726–30)

*Pamela* novel by Samuel Richardson (1740)

*Henry Earl of Moreland* John Wesley's abridgement of Henry Brooke, *The Fool of Quality* (1781)

*Goldsmith's History of Rome* Oliver Goldsmith's abridgement of *The Roman History* (1772)

Jane Eyre has not been allowed to sit with her Aunt Reed and cousins after dinner and is therefore reading Bewick's *History of British Birds* on her own when she is interrupted by her cousin, John. He picks on her and when he throws a book at her she hits her head on the door. Bleeding, she begins calling him names, and they get into a fight. His sisters, Eliza and Georgiana, run for Mrs Reed who comes in with the nursemaid, Bessie, and her servant, Abbot. Jane is taken away to 'the red-room' (p. 18).

## COMMENTARY

This chapter is one of the earliest accounts given by a child from a child's point of view in English fiction. Though it is actually being narrated in retrospect by the mature Jane Rochester several years after the close of Volume III, Chapter 11, it nonetheless provides us with a highly suggestive portrait of Jane Eyre's childish thoughts and feelings.

In the 'Folds of scarlet drapery' and the 'drear November day' (p. 14) we find an early example of the kind of visual contrast that is characteristic of the novel. The references to Bewick help disclose Jane's state of mind. The book is full of sublime images of shipwrecks, storms, Arctic wastes, high mountain reaches, death and disaster. However, Master Reed owns the books and 'the book-shelves', or as he says, 'will do in a few years' (p. 17), which therefore work symbolically to suggest that even though a girl may understand what's written, conventionally it is the boy who will grow up to be the legitimate heir in control of the household's documents, wills and deeds, regardless of his learning and nature. Moreover, her inferior position within the Reed family is made brutally clear through her fight with John. Written authority is backed up in his case by physical and verbal violence, so that he literally 'throws the book' at Jane. Property ownership is manifestly masculine. Master Reed rules by might and right. But, John's introduction also foreshadows his rather unfortunate end in Volume II, Chapter 6.

## CHAPTER 2

- Jane is locked in the red-room.

Miss Abbot and Bessie lock Jane in the 'red-room' (p. 20). Jane is initially angry, but soon becomes frightened as dusk falls. She thinks that the room is haunted and that her uncle, Mr Reed, who died in the room is about to come for her. She screams out in terror and Miss Abbot and Bessie come to see what is wrong, but Jane's aunt leaves her in the room for another hour. Jane passes out.

### COMMENTARY

In this chapter the supernatural mixes with mundane detail about the Reeds, Jane's origin and background. She is just ten and her fear of the 'red-room', connected as it is with death, seems quite natural. In addition to the child's point of view, however, we are also given a privileged insight into her position by the adult Jane who looks back and reflects on the scene.

The fact that Jane is described as 'a mad cat' (p. 19) and is made to sit fixedly on a chair as part of her punishment allows us to draw parallels between Jane and Mrs Rochester. We also learn that Jane

**GLOSSARY**
**cover** deceitfulness
**Marseilles** stiff cotton fabric
**race** blood-relations

**QUESTION**
What seems to make Jane so unacceptable to her 'superiors'?

**CHECK THE BOOK**
For more on the sexual imagery of *Jane Eyre* see E. Figes *Sex and Subterfuge: Women Writers to 1850* (1982).

can be quite superstitious as well as passionate, and she battles with both tendencies throughout the course of the novel.

This chapter can also be read symbolically as Jane's transition from girlhood into the early stages of womanhood. Jane's experiences at Gateshead represent a typically Victorian education in which an ardent girl is taught how to become a passive and restrained woman. In Charlotte Brontë's work the colour red, which connotes fire, is normally associated with sexuality – white and coldness with its absence – her being made to sit in 'the red-room' is therefore indicative of her entry into adolescence. Through this experience Jane also learns that she will be subject to unjust and oppressive punishments and that she cannot retreat into childhood any more – she cannot go back to the nursery. It is only once she faints, in others words, submits fully to her circumstances, that she is taken out of the room. After this she is treated a delicate creature, as a good woman should be.

## CHAPTER 3

- Jane says that she would like to go to school.

Jane wakes up to find that the servants' apothecary, Mr Lloyd, has been called to look at her. Bessie tries to cheer her up, but Jane can be tempted by neither tarts nor books. Mr Lloyd asks her why she is so sad and she tries to explain: 'I cry because I am miserable … I was shut up in a room where there is a ghost, till after dark' (p. 31). He asks her if she would like to leave and though she would not like to go to her father's family – whom she assumes are poor – she says she would like to go to school.

## COMMENTARY

We find out more about Jane's mother and Bessie's ballad reflects Jane's own condition as a 'poor orphan child' (p. 29). Bessie's story about the 'great, black dog' (p. 27) is picked up in Chapter 12, and the idea that all the fairies have left England is reiterated in

### GLOSSARY

**apothecary** a medical practitioner who was cheaper than a physician and not supposed to be paid for medical treatment, often acted as a kind of early General Practitioner at this time

**I ought to forgive … did** reference to Luke 23:34

**Gulliver's Travels** satire by Jonathan Swift (1726)

**In the days … ago** popular song, Edward Ransford (c.1840)

**My feet … child** unknown ballad

**backboards** devices meant to improve the way you sit or stand

**toad** general insult

**CONTEXT**

The Apothecaries Act of 1815 regulated the provision of medicine and medical advice, but there was an ongoing conflict between the physicians and the apothecaries about who should dispense medicine and who should provide medical treatment.

Chapter 13. We can therefore begin to guess that Bessie is very important to Jane. The nursemaid does in fact seem to care for Miss Eyre after all, and this sets the tone for their reconciliation in Chapter 4. However, her unconventional appearance not simply her outlandish behaviour will clearly remain a problem for Jane given the other servant, Abbot's opinion that she could be pitied 'if she were a nice, pretty child'. Even Bessie allows that 'a beauty like Miss Georgiana would be more moving in the same condition' (p. 34). Successful femininity clearly requires good looks.

Because we only ever receive information from Jane's point of view and because we get to know her deepest thoughts and feelings we tend to assume that she is a reliable narrator, but she is not always a sympathetic character. She is a precocious girl and there are moments when the reader feels quite sorry for Mrs Reed. Jane's initial response to the plight of the poor and her adult reflection on this serve to remind us that she is still just a child, brought up by the indolent and snobbish Reeds. She also maintains some of this attitude given her later treatment of the Rivers' servant in Volume III, Chapter 3. Given her use of the word 'caste' rather than 'class', it seems Jane sees the social divide as insuperable and the idea of crossing it quite taboo. This has racial connotations.

**GLOSSARY**

**waited** awaited

**stirred my corruption** (dialect) made me angry

**graven image** (biblical) idol

**traffic** trade

**to take ... flesh** Ezekiel, 11;19 and 36:26

**Child's Guide** based on a monthly tract, *The Children's Friend*

**racy** high quality

**onding on snaw** from Walter Scott, *The Heart of Midlothian*, 'pelting with snow'

## CHAPTER 4

- Jane meets Mr Brocklehurst, wins a psychological battle against her aunt and makes up with Bessie.

It is decided that Jane shall go to school. Jane continues to stand up for herself and starts to talk back to her aunt, who tells her cousins to stay away from her. Though the arrangements for sending Jane away seem to take a long time, she finally meets her future headmaster, Mr Brocklehurst, 'a black pillar! ... straight, narrow, sable-clad' (p. 40). Deeply upset when her aunt sullies her reputation, Jane tells Mrs Reed what she thinks of her. Mrs Reed is frightened and Jane exults in her first real victory over her aunt.

Jane, still overexcited, goes out into the garden and when Bessie comes to fetch her, Jane makes up with the nurse who likes the girl's new-found self-confidence.

## COMMENTARY

We are never surprised by Jane's behaviour as we move through the novel because the foundation is laid for every action and response. Jane's dislike of the company who turn up for Christmas prefigures her uneasiness at the arrival of guests at Thornfield in Volume II, Chapter 2. Though Jane swears never to call Mrs Reed 'aunt' again, when she does so, in Volume II, Chapter 6, she is quite self-conscious about it. We see all the characters in the novel from Jane's point of view and a perfect example of this can be found in the way our opinion of Bessie changes as Jane begins to see her differently.

Mr Brocklehurst is described by Jane as if he were the big bad wolf from 'Little Red Riding Hood', 'what a great nose! and what a mouth! and what large, prominent teeth!' (p. 41).

This reflects the influence of Bessie's stories on Jane and the child's point of view, but the implication is also that Mr Brocklehurst is a liar so that when he says Mrs Reed is 'judicious' (p. 43), and that he is consistent we should not believe him. Jane's replies to his questions about the Bible, heaven and hell are supposed to imply criticism of his highly conventional theology. However, they also suggest that Jane has not read the Gospels, which would have taught her to forgive those who harm her, as Helen Burns points out in Chapter 6.

## CHAPTER 5

- Jane goes to school.

Jane leaves Gateshead on 19 January. She arrives at Lowood school in the dark, rain and wind. She is so tired and overexcited that she cannot eat any supper. The next day the girls sit down to breakfast

**CHECK THE BOOK**

For an interesting comparative selection of fairy tales from around the world, ancient and modern, including Red Riding Hood, see *The Virago Book of Fairy Tales* (1990) and *The Second Book of Virago Fairy Tales* (1992) both edited by Angela Carter.

**CONTEXT**

Bessie tells Jane that she 'should be bolder' (p. 48), which is unusual as Jane's behaviour is often quite **'melodramatic'**.

**GLOSSARY**

**mess** prepared dish

**irids** plural of iris

**front** forehead

***Rasselas*** Samuel Johnson, *Rasselas* (1759), didactic romance about the aims of human life

**rusty** rancid

**CONTEXT**

In 1846, *Punch*, a widely read if essentially metropolitan middle-class satirical magazine, proposed (tongue-in-cheek) that there should be some kind of formal training for governesses, which recognised their unique social standing as peculiarly 'uncomfortable, though, like a certain process to which eels are subjected, nothing when anyone is used to it'.

but the porridge is burnt so they cannot eat it. Much to their surprise the superintendent, Miss Temple, therefore decides to serve the girls lunch. During her first day Jane meets another pupil who tells her about the school, its principles and its teachers.

## COMMENTARY

This chapter sets the scene for the Lowood section of the book and the next stage in Jane's life. It is therefore largely **expository**; much of the information is provided by the dialogue that takes place between Jane and the other pupil – Helen Burns. The harsh regime at the school is indicated by the cold weather. It also seems to parallel a description of the kind of school for governesses that *Punch* described in 1846. For example, the 'novices, during leisure hours, are to sit in separate apartments accessible to all of the servants, who, however, will not be allowed to wait upon them, or bring them any refreshment, if hungry from the insufficiency of their meals'. The exact nature of the regime is modelled by the school's garden. Though it is wide, it is enclosed by high walls and a large number of 'little beds … assigned as gardens for the pupils to cultivate' (p. 58). This is based on the Victorian idea that through gardening a child may learn good behaviour, but it also suggests that at Lowood it is believed that nature should and will be tamed. This becomes explicit in Chapter 7. Helen Burns's character is suggested by her choice of reading matter: *Rasselas*.

**GLOSSARY**

**stops** punctuation

**mark** embroider

**'the Bible bids us … evil'** based on Christ's sermon on the mount, Matthew 5–7

**'like Felix … convenient season'** Acts 24

**'Love your enemies … use you'** Matthew 5:44

**'the time … corruptible bodies'** I Corinthians 15:50–3

## CHAPTER 6

- Jane begins her career at Lowood.

Jane is enrolled as a member of the fourth class and begins her lessons. As she sits sewing, she sees her new friend participating in a history lesson. It appears that the girl, Burns, is being picked on by the teacher, Miss Scatcherd, even though the girl is very good at the subject. Though the water was frozen so that the girl could not have washed, for instance, Mrs Scatcherd says to Burns: 'You dirty, disagreeable girl! you have never cleaned you nails this morning!' (p. 64). At one point Burns is flogged, but takes it stoically. In the evening, Jane speaks to Burns and finds out that her first name is Helen. Jane asks her why she puts up with Miss Scatcherd's bullying and she explains the principles of endurance, duty and self-sacrifice to Jane, as based on the New Testament Gospels.

## COMMENTARY

The chapter largely consists of the conversation that takes place between Jane and Helen. Though this dialogue covers some complex theological ground, it is nonetheless quite naturalistic and provides us with a deep insight into Helen's character. Helen offers one solution to Jane's problem – the need to quell her passionate nature – and Jane does learn from her, as we begin to see in the following chapters. But Helen's faith is also essentially inward-looking, as indicated by her tendency to slip into reverie, and potentially death-willing; she looks forward to death as an elevation, 'I live in calm, looking to the end' (p. 70).

Jane meanwhile has been sent out from Gateshead, literally, into the cold. We know that the school is essentially repressive not only because of the behaviour of the teachers, but also because of the wintry setting – passion, indeed life, has been brought to a standstill. As we saw in the previous chapter, the gardens may contain flowers in the future – the girls may grow up to be pretty young women – but for the moment they have been frozen solid. A psychological reading would associate this with the endless waste of adolescence, as is also suggested by Jane's comment in the next chapter that she is having an 'irksome' time struggling 'with difficulties in habituating myself to new rules and unwonted tasks' (Ch. 7, p. 1). The cheapskate way in which the school is run is not only indicated through the girls' food, but also the use of rushlights.

> **CONTEXT**
>
> Stoicism includes the idea that life is best lived without the more extreme or violent feelings, the best way to achieve such freedom is through virtuous living. This philosophy is derived from several Classical, Greek, thinkers.

> **QUESTION**
>
> To what extent is Brontë attacking Evangelicalism?

> **CONTEXT**
>
> Brocklehurst is one of many Evangelicals represented negatively in nineteenth-century fiction. Others include Murdstone in Charles Dickens' *David Copperfield* and Slope in Anthony Trollope's *Barchester Towers*.

## CHAPTER 7

- Mr Brocklehurst tells the other school girls that Jane is a liar.

It is winter and all the girls suffer from the cold and hunger,

## GLOSSARY

**starved** frozen

**'the fifth, sixth … Matthew'** chapters that contain the sermon on the mount

**Eutychus** Acts 2:9–10, Eutychus falls asleep during one of St Paul's sermons and apparently falls to his death from a window, but is revived

**'Coming Man'** man likely to achieve eminence

**take up their cross** Mark 8:34

**man shall not live by bread alone … God** Matthew 4:4

**'if ye suffer … happy are ye'** Luke 6:21 and I Peter 3:14

**Grace** idea that God will redeem certain individuals and not others

**cup and platter** Matthew 13:25–6

**'kingdom is not of this world'** John 18:36

**false front** hairpiece

**'kneels before Juggernaut'** suggests that Jane prays to the Hindu god Krishna

**'even as the Jews … round her'** John 5:2–4

especially when they walk to church. The big girls hog the fire and take most of the little girls' food. Eventually the proprietor, Mr Brocklehurst, visits the school. He criticises Miss Temple for giving the girls lunch, picks on one of the girls, Julia Severn, for having naturally curly hair, even though his own daughters curl theirs artificially, and as soon as he sees Jane makes her sit in front of the whole school while he calls her a liar.

## COMMENTARY

To continue the focus on the sexual symbolism of the novel, we can see from the fact that the older girls stand closer to the fire than the younger, that the older girls are symbolically that bit closer to sexual maturity.

Jane's conflict with Mr Brocklehurst was **foreshadowed** in Volume I, Chapter 4. Mr Brocklehurst never lives up to his Evangelical principles and his character is formed in direct opposition to that of the other clergyman in the novel, St John Rivers. Brocklehurst is described (in Chapter 4) as 'a black pillar' (p. 40), whereas St John is 'marble' (Vol. III, Ch. 9, p. 457); Brocklehurst is a hypocrite, unlike St John who is ruthlessly consistent and as 'inexorable as death' (Vol. III, Ch. 5, p. 408).

Brocklehurst's inconsistency is made clear in his attack on Julia Severn and the entrance of his fashionably dressed wife and daughters. Eva Figes, a feminist critic who develops a psychological interpretation of the novel, has pointed out that the incident when Brocklehurst demands that Julia has her hair cut can be read as an instance of castration. The frozen world of Lowood thus equates to the castration phase. But, even setting this aside, Brocklehurst's worldview certainly becomes abundantly clear when he insists that the girls neither 'conform to the world' nor 'to nature' (p. 75). His religious principles are clearly impossible to live up to. Moreover, he looks to a higher state of being in 'Grace' i.e. at one with God, yet his way of brining this about is to maim God's creation. Beyond this, it is implied that this is the worst of all Christian worlds especially for women. Jane is falsely accused as she was in Chapter 1 and begins to panic as she did in Chapter 2, but by this point, thanks to Helen Burns' help and Miss Temple's example, Jane proves that she can control her emotions and take her punishment.

## CHAPTER 8

- Jane recovers her reputation.

After the school is dismissed, Jane is left alone and breaks down in tears. Her friend Helen comes to comfort her and when Miss Temple finds them she takes them to her room. Miss Temple takes Helen and Jane under her wing for the evening, and Jane is awed by Helen's knowledge. When Helen reads from Virgil she finds her 'organ of Veneration ... expanding with every line' (p. 86) read by Helen Burns. Jane tells her story to Miss Temple who writes to Mr Lloyd, the apothecary, for corroboration. When he writes back, she gets the whole school together and publicly clears Jane's reputation. Jane is promoted to a higher class and goes on to learn French and drawing.

## COMMENTARY

Charlotte and her sisters, like many radical – also Christian – middle-class intellectuals, subscribed to phrenology, and we can see how this worked itself out in her writing here. A pseudo-scientific practice, phrenology relied on empirical observation and the close measurement of a person's skull; their behaviour was supposed to be predictable given the shape and size of various 'organ's'. For example, the 'organ of Individuality' was believed to be in the middle of the lower part of the forehead. A person with a well-developed organ of Individuality would be a close observer of material details and have a great aptitude for natural history. The 'organ of Veneration' was connected with religious worship, but also an individual's inclination to look up to their superiors and to be charitable.

Helen's conversation with Jane shows that self-reliance can come from faith; self-respect and individuality are stressed here above all

**GLOSSARY**

**Barmecide supper** fantasy feast

**Cuyp-like** after the seventeenth-century Dutch landscape painter Albert Cuyp

**currently** fluently

**organ of Veneration** term from phrenology, the nineteenth-century practice of linking the skull's features to an individual's character

**Etre** the infinitive of the French verb 'to be'

**'Better is a dinner ... therewith'** Proverbs 15:17

**CONTEXT**

Even the minor character's names often reflect their temperament and interests. For example, 'Miss Temple' is quite saintly compared to the harsh 'Miss Scatcherd' who has a name that is evocative of scratches and shards.

else. The fact that Jane takes some of this teaching on board becomes clear in her visit to Gateshead and flight from Thornfield later on in the novel. When she comes to tell her story to Miss Temple we can see that Jane has already learnt to control some of her worst excesses thanks to Helen. And she finds that she can accommodate the privations of Lowood with the help of her new friends. Helen exemplifies the Christian ideal of turning one's cheek, forgiving one's enemies and meek endurance. She is a model of morality and of learning, but Jane is doubtful about the validity of Helen's example 'in the tranquillity she imparted there was an alloy of inexpressible sadness' (p. 82). Helen's faith makes her turn away from life and Helen's subsequent illness and death is **foreshadowed** several times.

## CHAPTER 9

- Helen Burns dies.

As winter gives way to spring, so most of the pupils begin to fall ill. More than half of them need nursing and the rest are left to look after themselves. Jane remains fairly well and can play in the spring sunshine, but many of the girls die and Helen becomes very sick from typhus. One evening Jane slips in to visit Helen, determined to see her friend before she dies. They talk a little and Jane is amazed by Helen's faith. Helen asks Jane to stay with her and as they sleep so Helen dies.

## COMMENTARY

In this chapter we see the first direct reference to the reader 'True, reader' (p. 91). This is a device which recurs several times throughout the remainder of the novel, the last being 'Reader, I married him' (Vol. III, Ch. 12, p. 498). This device creates a close bond between the narrator and the reader and draws the latter into the story. These petitions to the reader always come at moments of heightened intensity or action, often adding detail to a relationship or Jane's thoughts at that moment. In this case it acts as a supplement to the narrative, and highlights just how important Helen Burns is to Jane.

The conversation is convincing and naturalistic and there is considerable **pathos** in Helen's death. Helen is doomed to die young and her faith is shaped by this. As suggested in Chapter 6, Helen's religion is death-willing, she expects to be happier dead than alive, and Jane cannot understand this. Death and sickness are contrasted very sharply in this chapter with health and the will to live, both in the girls' environment and in their beliefs. In the morning Jane is merely sleeping while Helen is starkly '– dead' (p. 96).

We can read Helen Burns as Jane's *alter ego* – following the association of 'Burns' with fire and passion, she can be seen as that side of Jane that Jane must learn to repress in order to survive in Victorian society. Helen has survived in the hostile, frigid world of Lowood by going inside herself, by daydreaming, but this is not enough and she is burned up (by fever). She works as Jane's *alter ego* because this happens just as Jane begins to control her feelings, and once Helen dies Jane is much more easily schooled. It is only as an adult, married woman that Jane can resurrect this part of herself, as we can see from the final few lines. 'Her grave … for fifteen years … was only covered by a grassy mound; but now a gray [sic.] marble tablet marks the spot, inscribed with her name, and the word "Resurgam"' (p. 96).

## CHAPTER 10

- The school is reformed.
- When Miss Temple marries, Jane decides to advertise and is offered a job.

The outbreak of typhus leads to an enquiry into the running of Lowood and the school is reformed. Jane stays there a further eight years, six as a pupil and two as an assistant teacher. After Miss

---

**CONTEXT**

Jane says typhus 'breathed' (p. 89) through Lowood. At this time disease was often supposed to be propagated by bad air, called 'miasma'. One of the leading medical practitioners of the day therefore declared: 'All smell is, if it be intense, immediate acute disease; and eventually we may say that, by depressing the system and rendering it susceptible to the action of other causes, all smell is disease.' (Edwin Chadwick, 1846).

**GLOSSARY**

**stimulus** stimulation

**watch** stay awake

**plucked** failed exam

What has Jane learned during her time at Lowood?

**CONTEXT**

Bessie effectively asks Jane to show off her 'accomplishments'. It was deemed important at this time for a young lady to have acquired 'accomplishments', which generally consisted of decorative but essentially useless skills such as playing the piano and watercolour painting. A very well-educated girl like Jane Eyre would also have studied at least one foreign language, but she should also be able to entertain in 'polite' society.

Temple leaves, in order to marry a clergyman, Jane realises that it is time to go out into the world at large. She advertises for a new post and receives a letter from a Mrs Fairfax offering her a situation looking after a girl under ten at £30 a year, double her Lowood salary. She gets her references from the school committee and her new place is secured. As she waits for the carrier to collect her trunk Bessie arrives. Bessie tells Jane what has been happening at Gateshead and says that seven years ago a Mr Eyre, Jane's uncle, had visited the hall looking for her, but had had to go abroad on business. The next day, Jane leaves for her new job.

## COMMENTARY

The chapter opens with a discussion of the form of the novel, the observation that 'this is not to be a regular autobiography' (p. 97) in order to explain that eight years pass at Lowood before the next series of events unfold.

After the dramatic conclusion of the last chapter, here the early part of Jane's life is neatly tied up. She reflects on her time at Lowood, we are reminded of the characters she lived with at Gateshead, and a new character, Mr Eyre, is introduced. Jane is about to enter a new phase of her life. The chapter captures a moment at which Jane suddenly seems to grow psychologically. The use of repetition – 'I desired liberty; for liberty I gasped; for liberty I uttered a prayer' (p. 99) – is demonstrative of Jane's strength of feeling. This language also draws on the, still quite radical, language and concept of liberty drawn from the French Revolution, a language that women like Mary Wollstonecraft in her *Vindication of the Rights of Woman* (1792) had fought at the time to be extended to women, and one which was still seen to be more applicable to the (male) individual. It is therefore quite telling that she settles in the end for 'a new servitude' (p. 99). As she throws off her Lowood training, Jane suddenly realises that she has the inner resources to escape and 'surmount' (p. 99) the blue peaks that she sees ahead of her, a light sublime touch.

The heart of the novel lies in Jane's descriptions of what is going on in her own mind and her feelings, especially 'conscience' and 'passion', are often given their own voice. In this instance a 'kind fairy' seems to tell her what to do to get a new situation. These moments of **personification** help us to understand why Jane acts as she does. The use of the word also **foreshadows** Rochester's descriptions of Jane once she has her new job – see Chapter 14.

Jane's demonstration of her musical artistic talent, prefigures her doing the same later at Thornfield in Chapter 13. She has all the skills required of a governess, and, later a schoolmistress, but her drawings and paintings in particular represent her creativity. Later, it is her name on one of her drawings, see Volume III, Chapters 6 to 7, that gives away her identity to St John Rivers, suggesting a strong link between her artistic and her true selves.

## CHAPTER 11

- Jane arrives at Thornfield Hall.

Jane has reached Millcote and the chapter opens as she waits to be met by someone from Thornfield Hall. She finally arrives late at night, and is met by Mrs Fairfax. Mrs Fairfax is very cordial and Jane feels quite comfortable in her new place. The next day she learns that a Mr Rochester is master of the house and that her pupil, Miss Adèle Varens, is his ward. Mr Rochester seldom visits the hall, but he is well liked and respected. Jane is shown over the house and while descending from the attic hears an eerie laugh.

By this point Jane Eyre has become an accomplished young lady, as suggested by Bessie in the last chapter, however, as a governess she is nonetheless placed in an awkward social position. In this chapter Jane leaves her childhood and schooling behind her and enters adolescence 'inexperienced youth' (p. 108). The opening lines – 'A new chapter in a novel' (p. 108) – make it clear that we are reading a work of fiction, despite the book's subtitle, 'An Autobiography'. However, because of this clarification we are no longer sure that we know who our narrator is; is it still Jane Eyre or someone else?

### GLOSSARY

**romantic** wild landscape

**canzonette** short light song

**'La Ligue ... Fontaine'** one of the animal fables of the French author Jean de la Fontaine

**cabinet piano** upright piano

**spar** crystal

**Tyrian-dyed** coloured a reddish purple

**Parian** white marble

**Hebrew ark** with gilt winged cherubs, see Exodus 25, 36, 37, I Kings 6:29–35

**'after life's ... well'** Shakespeare, *Macbeth* III. 2. 23

**Bluebeard's castle** reference to fairy story

**syllabic** speech-like

### QUESTION

How representative is Jane's position as governess?

**CONTEXT**

'Bluebeard' is a fairy story in which a young wife is allowed to enter any room she wants in her husband's castle except one. When he leaves the castle on business one day she takes the keys and investigates. In the room she finds the bodies of his previous wives.

**GLOSSARY**

'Gytrash' huge black, shaggy dog from folklore that appears in churchyards and lonely lanes at dusk. If it looks you in the eye, you are warned of the death of a relative or friend

**mask** form

'Like heath ... away' Thomas Moore, 'Fallen is the throne...' ll. 19–20

'too easy chair' Alexander Pope, *Dunciad* IV. 343

## COMMENTARY

Several new characters are introduced – Mrs Fairfax, Adèle Varens, Mr Rochester, Grace Poole – and numerous events are **foreshadowed**. It is particularly worth paying close attention to the description of the house and grounds, as there are many close associations between them and their master, Mr Rochester. Thornfield itself, reflecting its name, has 'an array of mighty old thorn trees, strong, knotty, and broad as oaks' (p. 114) in its grounds, while the garden is visually linked to the fields that surround the estate. This suggests that Thornfield has its wilder aspects, though a great house this is not all neatly-clipped domesticity, while the connotation of freedom in this also contrasts with the walled regimented garden at Lowood. Jane sleeps well in her small room, but the rest of the house is eerily empty without its master and seems to harbour secrets. At the end of the chapter the description of the attic, the reference to an eerie laugh and the allusion to Bluebeard add to the **Gothic** tone of the Thornfield section of the text and foreshadow the discovery that Rochester is already married to a madwoman whom he keeps locked away on the third floor.

## CHAPTER 12

- Jane meets her master, Mr Rochester.

Jane settles in. When she is bored she goes for walks or climbs to the attic and longs for excitement. One day she walks to Hay to deliver a letter. It is very cold and as she rests she sees a horse and rider slip on some ice. She helps the man remount his horse and continues on her errand. When she returns to the hall she discovers that the man she helped was her master, Mr Rochester.

## COMMENTARY

Jane's sojourns in the attic help form an imaginative link between Jane Eyre and Mrs Rochester, as in the 'red-room'. If Jane fell victim to her passions, or even if she became mistress of the house, she could become as degenerate as her rival. As we can see from her assumption that Rochester's dog is the Gytrash, Jane's imagination is full of fiends, and the fact that she is sensitive to omens becomes particularly important in Volume III, Chapter 9. The scene in which Jane and Rochester meet for the first time is dramatic and its outcome, when he finds that 'necessity compels me to make you useful' (p. 131), **foreshadows** his ultimate physical dependence on her, Volume III, Chapter 12. Again, it is significant that they meet over ice, and that later she finds the fires lit at Thornfield where the grates had stood empty. Indeed, until he comes, to return to Thornfield is 'to return to stagnation' (p. 132). Jane does not want the trappings of conventional femininity, as she says herself, she is 'becoming incapable of appreciating' the 'very privileges of security and ease' (p. 132) her job at Thornfield have given her. Under his power she will begin to melt and unlearn much of her Lowood reserve, while for her he will renounce his wandering ways.

## CHAPTER 13

- Mr Rochester quizzes Jane about her past.

Thornfield is enlivened by visitors who come to do business with Mr Edward Fairfax Rochester. At the end of the day Jane and Adèle are invited to take tea with the master who interrogates Jane about her history, asks her to play the piano and requires her to show him her sketches.

## COMMENTARY

Mr Rochester is a Romantic, almost Byronic, figure who, in this chapter, is shown to be forceful and independent; in this respect he is in part Jane's *alter ego*. A Byronic hero is so called after the poet Byron, and this term is especially apt as it refers to a charismatic yet brooding and misanthropic character. Having travelled, seeking exotic adventure, such a character often harbours a guilty secret, about which he has no real shame. A Byronic hero is proud, sets

**CONTEXT**

The popularity of the novel leads it to have many fans, something commented on by Jasper Fforde in his humorous tale *The Eyre Affair: a novel* in which the protagonist, Thursday Next, enters the novel and watches this scene under cover.

**GLOSSARY**

**prenomens** first and second names

**piquant** stimulating

**'men in green'** fairies always wear the colour green

**'head and front of his offending'** Shakespeare, *Othello* I. 3. 80

**'Approach the table'** bring the table closer

**copies** originals

**'The likeness ... none'** Milton, *Paradise Lost*, II. 666–73

**Latmos** mountain in Turkey (Besh Parmark), where, in classical legend, the goddess of the moon, Silene, fell in love with Endymion

## CONTEXT

Heathcliff in Emily Brontë 's *Wuthering Heights* (1847) is another classic example of a Byronic hero. *Wuthering Heights* was published just a month after *Jane Eyre*. The two novels were often assumed to be by the same author, and Charlotte Brontë worked hard to defend the reputation of her work from its association with her sister's, given that *Wuthering Heights* was generally seen as much more risqué.

himself apart from society's norms and values, but, despite being rebellious and quite menacing, remains fascinating to others. This, as we will see, exactly describes Rochester.

Jane and Rochester's convincing and witty banter brings both characters alive. She may have feminine accomplishments, but she is as unconventional and strong-minded as he is and can always match him blow for blow in any conversation. Rochester often refers to Jane as a fairy, a sprite and an imp, 'When you came on me in Hay Lane last night, I thought unaccountably of fairy tales,' (p. 139) but he eventually learns that he must respect her as an individual a marked departure from the literary (and social) conventions of the day.

Jane's paintings reflect the **Romantic** preoccupation with extreme, wild landscapes and exotica and echo the landscapes of the book she was reading in the opening chapter. As noted earlier, this is indicative of her true nature.

## CHAPTER 14

- Mr Rochester and Jane spar with each other.

After a few days Jane and Adèle are again called in to spend the evening with Rochester, who gives Adèle a box of toys and a dress. Jane and Edward engage in another sparring conversation, this time about his appearance, their relative social positions and morality.

## COMMENTARY

The chapter begins in a characteristically journalistic style. These descriptive passages draw us into the action, and are often highly suggestive. However, though the language used is simple and direct, and while, as in the last chapter, the dialogue is generally quite convincing and naturalistic, much of the tenor of the conversation that takes place here is evocative of fairy stories like 'The Beauty and the Beast'.

## GLOSSARY

**interlocutrice** companion in conversation

**nonnett** little nun

**'bad eminence'** Milton, *Paradise Lost*, II. 6

Jane and Rochester's conversations allow us to learn a lot about his character, attitudes and state of mind. The way in which the different characters speak usually reflects their education and station, and with respect to Adèle it is also indicative of her nationality and training. The extensive use of French in the novel adds veracity to Adèle's exchanges with Jane and makes Jane's own accomplishments more tangible.

Again, we have a phrenological moment when Rochester holds up the hair from his forehead in order for Jane to inspect his 'intellectual organs' though as he notes there is 'an abrupt deficiency where the suave sign of benevolence should have risen' (p. 150). It is on this basis that Jane implies he is no 'philanthropist', which suggests that his kindness towards her – in letting her sit with him after dinner, despite the difference in their stations – is not done out of charity. His statement that he bears 'a conscience' (p. 150) is perhaps born out by his attempt to save Bertha when the house burns down.

## CHAPTER 15

- Mr Rochester tells Jane a little of his past and Jane saves him from a fire.

Another conversation takes place between Jane and Rochester as they walk in the hall's grounds. This time he tells Jane Adèle's story. That night, Jane lies awake reflecting on their discussion. Jane no longer thinks that Rochester is ugly. Now he brightens up her life. When she goes to investigate a strange noise she discovers that Rochester's bed has been set alight. She puts the fire out. Rochester goes to find the arsonist and on his return Grace Poole's name is mentioned. Rochester prefers to compliment Jane on her actions rather than talk about the fire, however, and before they part he confesses that he feels a natural sympathy for her.

**CONTEXT**

Adèle, a French girl, has been sent to England for her education, but many young middle-class women were sent to boarding schools in France. This was done because French education was supposed to be strong in music and grammar, i.e. literature and conversation, requisites for feminine accomplishment.

**GLOSSARY**

**Apollo Belvidere** famous statue of Apollo in the Vatican

**hotel** town house

**dentelles** lace

**spoonie** demonstratively fond lover

**'Job's leviathan … habergeon'** Job 41:26

**'heart's core'** Shakespeare, *Hamlet* III. 2. 73

**extinguisher** of candle

**chicken in the pip** diseased chicken

**Beulah** an idyllic place, see Isaiah 62:4 and Bunyan, *The Pilgrim's Progress*

**CONTEXT**

The Medea legend is complex, but crucially Medea is a sorceress whose husband Jason eventually loses interest in her and marries someone else, Creusa. When Medea takes revenge, Creusa's father kills thirteen of Medea's fourteen children. In his play – *Medea* 431 BCE – Eurpides rewrote the tale reducing the number of children to two and saying she stabbed them.

## COMMENTARY

This chapter forms the end of the first volume and marks a clear alteration in Rochester and Jane's relationship. The fire foreshadows the destruction of Thornfield as outlined in Volume III, Chapter 10 and, with Jane's speculation about Rochester, generates a sense of suspense. Again, Rochester is shown to need Jane who seems to know him better than he knows himself. He seems unable to express himself, and his true feelings are revealed as he begins to lose fluency. We know Jane's hopes and fears because we are given a privileged insight into her innermost thoughts; we know his through conversation and what he does not say.

The fire symbolises raging passion, out of control, either Bertha's or Rochester's, doused by Jane's Christian temperance – she 'baptize[s] the couch' (p. 168) – though Rochester accuses her of being a 'witch, sorceress' (p. 169). This last image draws on Medea possibly a more apt description of Bertha Mason than Jane. Again, Bertha and Jane are linked imaginatively; though one sets and the other douses the fire, Rochester can hardly tell the difference.

**GLOSSARY**

**momentarily** moment by moment

**unvarnished tale** Shakespeare, *Othello*, I. 3. 90

# VOLUME II

## CHAPTER 1

- Jane tries to come to her senses.

The next morning Jane sees Grace Poole, the suspected arsonist, helping to restore Rochester's room. When Jane confronts her she warns Jane to keep her door locked at night. Jane is puzzled by this and hopes to ask Rochester about it. At tea-time she finds out that he has gone away to visit some fine friends. Mrs Fairfax describes some of the people he will meet and Jane realises that she has been foolish in thinking she could be one of his favourites. She paints a self-portrait called 'Portrait of a Governess, disconnected, poor, and plain' (p. 183).

## COMMENTARY

At the opening of Volume II, the suspense generated in the previous chapter is maintained while our curiosity is aroused by Jane's strange conversation with Grace. No-one is quite what they seem. Events in Volume II, Chapter 10 are foreshadowed when Grace warns Jane to lock her door. It becomes clear that Jane is falling in love with Rochester, and her method of handling him once they are engaged is suggested here in her cocksure pleasure at 'vexing and soothing him' (p.180). But in the meantime Jane is very hard on herself, calling herself a 'dupe', and 'Blind puppy' (p. 185). Several new characters are introduced and help highlight Jane's ambiguous social position. It is worth noting how she expresses her feelings through art, and how she holds the described beauty of Blanche Ingram up against her own mien. As suggested by the title she gives to her portrait, she cannot realistically hope to marry Rochester because of the difference in class, but, initially at least, Blanche is also described as the beau ideal of beauty and Jane is well aware that she cannot compete on these terms – see the earlier discussion between Bessie and Abbot about Jane's looks and their impact. In this case femininity is delineated through ugliness and its opposite. Jane quells her feelings, as she learned to do at Lowood. Rochester will use Blanche Ingram to make Jane jealous.

**CHECK THE BOOK**

For a study of the way in which *Jane Eyre* picks up on the image of and issues surrounding the governess see Mary Poovey, *Uneven Developments the Ideological Work of Gender in Mid-Victorian England* (1989).

---

**GLOSSARY**

**'a very pleasant ... trouble'** Psalms 46:1

**Mesrour** Executioner

**'Some natural tears she shed'** Milton, *Paradise Lost*, XII, 645

**'minois chiffonné'** with charming irregularity

**incubus** from the Latin for nightmare, something that weights heavily on the mind, but also a male demon that descends upon women as they sleep

**Dowager** lives independently on her dead husband's property    cont.

---

## CHAPTER 2

- Miss Ingram and friends visit Thornfield.

After a fortnight the party comes to stay at Thornfield. The house is prepared, extra servants are got in. During the preparations, Jane overhears part of a conversation about Grace Poole, but cannot make much sense of it as she is deliberately excluded from the mystery. The fine people soon arrive, the house is full of guests, servants, hustle and bustle. The next day, Jane and Adèle are invited to join the party after dinner. As the ladies chatter, as the men enter and as all engage in the evening's amusement, Jane watches. While

### CONTEXT

As Charlotte herself observed: 'None but those who had been in the position of a governess could ever realise that dark side of "respectable" human nature; under no great temptation to crime, but daily giving way to selfishness and ill-temper, till its conduct toward those dependent on it sometimes amounts to a tyranny of which one would rather be the victim than the inflicter.'

she does so she overhears a nasty conversation about governesses. When Jane slips away Rochester comes after her and insists that she join the party in the drawing room every evening until they go.

## COMMENTARY

The whole of this chapter repays close analysis, for example, what does Rochester want to say when he hesitates 'Good-night, my –' (p. 205)? Jane's hatred of company was **foreshadowed** in Volume I, Chapter 4 but in this instance we are provided with a slice of upper-class life, as observed by someone who sees herself as a social outcast. Again, the fact that Jane is in a socially anomalous position is important and adds piquancy to the conversation about governesses. '[Y]ou should hear mamma on the chapter of governesses. Mary and I have had ... a dozen at least in our day; half of them detestable and the rest ridiculous, and all incubi' (p. 200). This exchange plays on several issues surrounding the governess in the 1840s; the issue of cost, their morality and their ability to maintain standards, and their susceptibility. The governess, it was supposed, was liable to both madness and to seduction. The governess was therefore often despised by her social superiors. This was something that, as a governess, Charlotte Brontë was well aware of.

In this instance 'succubus' – from the Latin for 'to lie under', a female demon that descends upon a man as he sleeps – might be more apt than 'incubus' given recent events. The error goes to show Blanche Ingram's ignorance of the real situation and works as a possible comment on her obviously flawed education. Jane hides behind the curtain as she did in Volume I, Chapter 1, a position that reflects her marginalized status in both great houses, but in this case allows her, as narrator, privileged access to others' conversations.

The frequent use of the present tense gives Jane's descriptions immediacy and draws us into the scene. However, because Jane's narrative is written some years after the event she can also reflect more maturely and quite humorously on her adolescent attempts to 'master' herself and dismiss her highly inappropriate feelings. Because of this, **irony** clearly plays an important part in the whole of the novel.

Incidentally, Jane constantly refers to Rochester as her 'master' in a way which suggests that he in fact psychologically 'masters' her.

## CHAPTER 3

- A game of charades, a stranger and a gypsy.

The party stays on and engages in a variety of pastimes, including a game of charades. Jane is convinced that Rochester will marry Miss Ingram, 'for rank and connexions' (p. 211). While Rochester is absent a stranger, Mr Mason, calls to see him. While he waits for Rochester's return an old gypsy woman appears and insists on telling 'the gentry their fortunes' (p. 217). Eventually, all of the ladies go to her, including Jane.

### COMMENTARY

The stress of the chapter lies on appearances and disguises. The stage-like entrances and exits of the last chapter are played on in the game of charades, and in the dramatic arrival of the stranger and old gypsy woman. Jane's reflections on social convention and the necessity of marrying for love are important when she comes to consider St John Rivers' proposal in Volume III. More significantly, though, a marriage founded on charade – Rochester seems to specialise in mock marriages – and the arrival of a stranger are distinctly ominous.

Jane's opinion of Miss Ingram is quite haughty; though she acknowledges that the latter is her social superior. And, Jane asserts that she is not jealous – this is despite the best efforts of Rochester who seems determined to flirt quite outrageously – because she does not think Rochester loves the heiress and the heiress is all show. The reader might want to consider whether Jane is quite the reliable narrator in this instance, but it is quite telling that Jane can see Rochester, the man she loves, as capable of financial or political self-interest in this case, but not amorous self-interest later on.

**GLOSSARY**

**sacques, modes, lappets** all eighteenth-century items of women's dress

**pantomimes** mime or silent play acting

**Paynim** pagan

**bowstring** used by assassins

**'She hasted … to drink'** Genesis 2:4

**Bridewell** London prison

**old Mother Bunches** Mother Bunch was a byword for jests and 'old wives' tales'

**crock** (dialect) smut

**tinkler** tinker

**the old gentleman** the devil

**Sibyl** female prophet

**'I'm sure … not right'** Goldsmith, *Vicar of Wakefield*

**GLOSSARY**

**'nickered'** laughed

**blackaviced** dark-skinned

**'The passions may rage ... things'** Psalms, 2:1

**'Strong wind ... voice'** I Kings 19:11–12

**'the play is played out'** untraced quotation

**'Did I dream ... still?'** Keats, 'Ode to a Nightingale' ll. 79–80

**eld** old

**'Off, ye lendings!'** Shakespeare, *King Lear* III. 4. 111

**CONTEXT**

The gyspy fortune-teller episode plays on the dominant stereotype of the gypsy, while Roma or gypsies themselves remained a marginalized group. Though a treatise calling for the better treatment of gypsies was written by a Quaker, John Hoyland, in 1816, gypsies camping on the roadside were fined when the Turnpike Act of 1822 came into force.

## CHAPTER 4

- Jane and the gypsy.

Jane meets the gypsy who seems bent on asking her questions, rather than telling her fortune, which makes Jane suspicious. The gypsy reads Jane's face then asks her to go. Jane hesitates and realises that the gypsy is actually Mr Rochester. When he hears that Mr Mason has arrived in his absence he is stunned, but when everyone retires all seems well.

### COMMENTARY

Jane and the gypsy's conversation begins in a way that is again reminiscent of 'Little Red Riding Hood' this mirrors Jane's conversation with Mr Brocklehurst in Volume I, Chapter 4. 'You've a quick ear.' 'I have; and a quick eye and a quick brain' (p. 221). Contrast the 'gypsy's' assessment of Jane as 'cold', 'sick' and 'silly' (p. 222) with Jane's own insistence that she is 'disconnected, poor, and plain' (Vol. II, Ch. 1, p. 183). Notice how, as the conversation between them becomes more intimate Jane moves closer to the fortune-teller (Rochester) who stirs the fire to light her up, though she later complains 'the fire scorches me' (p. 226). This further suggests that Rochester kindles passion in Jane. His reading of her nature, of the way 'passions may rage furiously ... but judgement shall have the last word in every argument' (p. 227) tells us that he is a close observer and captures the essence of her character. Later, when she leaves Thornfield it is indeed because she listens to 'that still small voice which interprets the dictates of conscience' (p. 227). It is this sense of propriety that he tries to undermine, and which causes her to say of the penetrative interview 'it was not right' (p. 228). She is angry at Rochester for the loss of control this entails, at the way her story has been stolen from her by the gypsy. But, this is the most intimate scene between them so far. The unveiling of Mr Rochester is dramatically and symbolically significant, further developing the theme of charade. With the arrival of Mr Mason, we move closer to the mystery at the heart of Thornfield. Rochester's declaration that he has 'got a blow' (p. 229) so that he leans on her

echoes the scene when she helps him after the fall from his horse and **foreshadows** his later dependence on her.

## CHAPTER 5

- The company are woken by a scream and Jane nurses Mr Mason.

Jane hears a cry, struggle and a call for help. Once he has pacified his guests, Rochester asks Jane to follow him into the attic and leaves her to nurse Mr Mason who has been slashed by a knife. She and Mr Mason are sworn to silence while Rochester fetches a surgeon and while she waits Jane speculates about what has happened. As dawn comes Rochester returns and the doctor quickly dresses Mason's wounds. He is spirited away and Jane is left puzzling over events but Rochester begins one of his moral conversations. Finally he starts talking about marrying Miss Ingram.

The bloody mystery deepens. Because Jane is unable to follow any of the conversations that take place around her or what Rochester says to her, neither can we. The hall, which is always symbolically important, becomes more mysterious, more gothic. Notice how Thornfield and its owner, who still seems to be playing charades, are linked.

### COMMENTARY

Jane is morally direct and sure-footed; she will only 'obey' (p. 244) Rochester if it is right to do so and this becomes important at the end of the volume. The full moon is clearly associated with the lunatic antics of Mrs Rochester, who behaves like a vampire – picked up again in Volume II, Chapter 10. Despite original reports of her beauty, Miss Ingram is described here as 'a real strapper … big, brown and buxom' (p. 247) in other words she looks just like Mrs Rochester, whose room is directly above Jane's, and in many respects also behaves like Bertha before Edward married her. Rochester married Miss Mason for money and this is the only

**CHECK THE FILM**

The often gloomy atmosphere of Thornfield, in keeping with the novel's **Gothic** overtones, and its ominous overtones are captured very well by Franco Zeffirelli in his (1996) film adaptation.

reason, Jane believes, that he would marry Blanche Ingram. The fact that Bertha's room is directly above Jane's, however, also suggests a connection between Mrs Rochester and the governess – Jane is in danger of becoming like Bertha if she weds Rochester.

The horrors of the attic are contrasted with those of the garden in the early morning. The fresh 'old-fashioned flowers' (p. 243) flowers generate scent that evokes a sense of freedom and wild nature. Despite the April showers, the scene in the garden – especially the phrase 'You have passed a strange night, Jane' (p. 243) – evokes Shakespeare's *A Midsummer Night's Dream*, a motif that is more fully explored in Volume II, Chapter 8.

Where Jane calls to the Greek gods, she wishes for Ariel to speak to her in the 'breath' (p. 246) of the west wind. Jane will later hear the moon advise her to 'flee temptation' in Volume III, Chapter 1 (p. 358). Later still, she will hear Rochester's voice calling her back and Rochester will hear her reply.

## CHAPTER 6

- Jane dreams about a baby every night for a week.

Jane is unsettled by a recurring dream about an infant and sees it as a bad omen. She is summoned to Gateshead by her aunt who is very ill. Her cousin John has died in mysterious circumstances. Rochester is reluctant to let her go, but she finally gets a leave of absence. While talking to Rochester she asks him to find her another situation before he marries. Her arrival at Gateshead brings back memories; she is welcomed by Bessie though Miss Eliza and Miss Georgiana are less agreeable. Jane insists on seeing her aunt who is very confused. Some days later her aunt gives her a three-year-old letter from a John Eyre, her uncle, who wanted to adopt her. Jane refers to Mrs Reed as 'aunt' (p. 259), but despite Jane's attempts at kindness there can be no reconciliation. Mrs Reed dies.

## COMMENTARY

The chapter begins in reflective mood and moves on into the structure of 'The Beauty and the Beast'. We are filled in on the recent history of the Reeds, which provides a link back to Volume I and allows Jane to complete the business of her childhood. Her aunt's use of the third person of Jane – 'I have had more trouble with that child than any one would believe' (p. 260) – when she is talking to her, allows us to gain some understanding of Mrs Reed's point of view. Jane tries to behave as Helen Burns would have done, but learns that she must be true to herself and that people do not change in the way her religious schooling suggests that they should.

Jane's cousins represent two opposing kinds of conventional femininity, the kind whose sole aim is to marry to advantage, the other self-sacrificing and inclined to retreat from the world onto the moral high ground. Jane herself detests all things that smack of popish Catholicism, as opposed to good English Protestantism. Jane is a chauvinist. Though this can be read in part as being about Charlotte Brontë's faith, these anti-Catholic overtones fit in perfectly with the **Gothic** elements of the novel as a whole – eighteenth-century Gothic novels often being anti-Catholic.

The reference at the beginning of the chapter to 'Presentiments', 'sympathies' and 'signs' (p. 248) becomes particularly pertinent in Volume III, Chapter 9, but Jane's sensitivity to all kinds of omens is often used to **foreshadow** coming events and helps drive the plot, add **irony** and create suspense. Uncanny imagery and symbolism help pull the different parts of the novel together into an organic whole. Jane's uncle becomes important in Volume II, Chapter 11 and Volume III, Chapter 7.

**CONTEXT**

Jane has learned how to interpret dreams from Bessie, the servant, and this is a typical **Gothic** motif – in Gothic novels it is servants, especially old nursemaids, who generally teach their charges about folklore and the supernatural.

**CHECK THE BOOK**

To learn more about Charlotte Brontë's religious feeling see M. Thormahlen, *The Brontës and Religion* (1999).

## CHAPTER 7

- Jane realises that Thornfield and its master together make up 'home'.

**GLOSSARY**

**second-sight** ability to tell the future

A month later Jane leaves Gateshead. Georgiana eventually marries and Eliza finally takes the veil. When she returns to Thornfield, Jane is surprised by her feelings for Rochester and discloses that she would not really like to leave him again. There is a rumour that he is about to marry, but few preparations.

## COMMENTARY

A short interim chapter in which several loose ends are tied up. Eliza Reed has been shown to be quite heartless; she is focused on the small details of life – she works diligently to complete all the little jobs that she sets out to do, and is well aware of what constitutes proper and improper behaviour. But, she has no interest in the metaphysical, the spiritual or even the feeling aspects of human life; Eliza Reed is uncharitable and uncaring. Her freely made decision to go to a convent is therefore damning of the Catholic religion, especially as she is so successful in her vocation.

Jane returns to Thornfield which reappears under its pleasantest aspect and at the beginning of summer, an appropriate time and setting for courtship.

The use of the present tense, as Jane approaches Thornfield Hall, gives the whole scene immediacy.

## GLOSSARY

'Day its fervid ... wasted' Thomas Campbell, 'The Turkish Lady' l.5

lady-clock (dialect) lady-bird; (children's rhyme) 'Lady-bird, lady-bird fly away home, / Your house is on fire, / Your children all flown'

'morsel of bread, living water' (biblical) refers to communion

## CHAPTER 8

- Rochester proposes.

Jane meets Rochester as she walks in the grounds on Midsummer-eve, and he engages her in conversation. He says that she must leave Thornfield as he will soon marry. She begins to cry. They sit under the old chestnut tree and he suddenly confesses that he has no intention of marrying Miss Ingram at all, he actually wants to marry Jane. Jane doubts and quizzes, but finally accepts him. During the night a great storm splits the old chestnut tree in two.

## COMMENTARY

This provides us with the first climax of the novel. The setting is Edenic – again, semi-wild, old-fashioned flowers draw Jane's attention, as does Thornfield's place in the landscape as a whole – and includes allusions to Keats – a nightingale sings – as well as Shakespeare's *A Midsummer Night's Dream*, a play in which lovers are constantly tricked, turned around and bewitched by fairies. The language is heightened and passionate, quite journalistic where Jane cannot express her emotion, and the tone one of foreboding. Rochester's observation that a moth reminds him of a 'West Indian insect' (p. 280) gestures towards the final revelation that Rochester is married to a Creole. But, there is humour here too in Rochester's suggestion that Jane educate 'the five daughters of Mrs Dionysius O'Gall of Bitternutt Lodge' (p. 282). The fact that he is teasing her is made clear in the names 'O'Gall' and 'Bitterenutt', but this is quite subtle and she remains ignorant of his real intent.

Throughout the novel Thornfield and its grounds are closely associated with their master – we can see this in the way that the scent of Rochester's cigar mingles with that of the flowers – and the fact that the old tree is split in two is ominous, given that the tree is symbolic of Jane and Rochester's relationship. The storm also suggests that God will not pardon Rochester or sanction his actions – he is still in effect living a lie even though the charade of an engagement with Miss Ingram is over.

## CHAPTER 9

- Arrangements are made for the wedding.

The next day Rochester says that they will be married in a month. He wants to shower Jane with gifts and take her on a tour of Europe. Jane is wary and does not want to be flattered or dressed in jewels. Mrs Fairfax is not entirely easy about what has happened and is worried that something will go wrong. Jane, Adèle and

**CHECK THE NET**

Jane in part hopes to make a decision based on her phrenological skills; for a history of phrenology and further references go to **http://pages. britishlibrary.net/ phrenology/**

**CHECK THE BOOK**

For a detailed discussion of phrenology, which puts Charlotte Brontë's work in the context of Victorian psychological debate, see S. Shuttleworth *Charlotte Brontë and Victorian Psychology* (1996).

**CONTEXT**

Dress was seen as being indicative of a woman's morality in the nineteenth century; prostitutes were often said to wear 'finery' especially velvets, feathers and costume jewellery.

**GLOSSARY**

**mustard-seed** fairy in *A Midsummer Night's Dream*

**Hercules** in classical legend Hercules is enslaved by his love for Omphale

**Samson** Samson reveals the secret of his strength to Delilah, his mistress

**'gild refined gold'** *King John* IV, 2. 11

**Ashasuerus** Persian king who marries a poor Jewish girl, Esther

**'I lay ... soul'** Shakespeare, *Hamlet* III. 4. 145

**'the world ... lost'** Dryden, *All for Love, or the World well Lost*

**Danae** in classical legend, Danae is seduced by Zeus who appears as a shower of gold

**three-tailed bashaw** Turkish ruler

**'Yes, bonny ... tyne'** Burns, 'The bonny wee thing', 11. 3–4

**The truest love ... loved am I** the song is Bronte's

Rochester go to Millcote where Jane and Rochester tussle over dresses and trinkets. Jane determines to write to her uncle in order to secure her independence and she insists that she continue as governess for the month of their engagement. That evening she gets him to sing to her and she consistently keeps him at arm's length during the rest of their courtship.

## COMMENTARY

The fact that there is trouble ahead is clearly **foreshadowed,** which adds suspense to what is otherwise a straightforward romance. The fact that the narrator can drop hints that Rochester is still hiding something – 'as if well pleased at seeing a danger averted' (p. 294) – and the fact that Jane can ignore them can make us feel a little uncomfortable until we remember that the narrative is being told by an older and wiser Jane some time after the event.

Rochester takes up Jane's psychological usage of 'master' when he says 'you master me' (p. 293). Also notice the explicit reference to Samson's story, which is referred to obliquely several times in the rest of the novel. Later, St John comments that Jane is 'original' in a similar way to Rochester in Volume III, Chapter 6 and it is worth remembering her joke with Rochester about becoming a missionary when St John Rivers' plans for her are revealed. There is a distinct contrast in Rochester's attitude to clothes a jewellery in the penultimate chapter, 'The third day from this must be our wedding day,' he declares. 'Never mind fine clothes and jewels, now: all that is not worth a fillip' (Vol. III, Ch. 11, p. 495).

Songs and ballads are inserted regularly into the text in their entirety throughout the book and bear close examination for their themes and their reception. For example, after being imprisoned in the red-room Jane finds Bessie's gypsy song saddening where she had once enjoyed it at as an adventurous tale.

## CHAPTER 10

- Jane sees a spectre.

As Jane waits for Rochester's return from business she is disturbed by an event that happened the previous night. As she walks in the grounds she passes by the old chestnut tree. Eventually, Rochester arrives and, at midnight, she tells him that the previous night an apparition came to her room, and tore the veil he had given her. Rochester assures her that she merely saw Grace Poole, and sends her to sleep with Adèle in the nursery.

### COMMENTARY

A **Gothic** chapter, full of foreboding. Notice the motif of the little child and her dream that Thornfield is reduced to a shell as examples of prescience. Jane's thoughts on contemplating the ruin of the chestnut tree **foreshadow** her feelings when reunited with Rochester at the end of the novel. 'I think, scathed as you look, … there must be a little sense of life in you yet, rising out of that adhesion at the faithful honest roots' (p. 309–10). It is only after Rochester has been 'scorched' that Jane can come to him, for the moment he remains 'ardent and flushed' (p. 313) with desire, in danger of burning out of control. There is **irony** in her refusal to use the luggage labels because 'Mrs Rochester' does not yet exist, especially when Mrs Rochester tears Jane's own veil, though at least this allows Jane to wear the plain veil she preferred to the excessive one he sent for from London. There are also references to earlier events in the novel, particularly in the red-room and Bertha's attack on Mr Mason.

This is the first clear sight we have of Bertha Rochester, who until this point has made her presence felt largely by wails, fire and violence. She is described as 'discoloured' and 'savage' 'purple' with lips 'swelled and dark' and 'bloodshot eyes' (p. 317). Jane's association of Bertha with a vampire, based on this appearance, was a commonplace in the nineteenth century – descriptions of vampires closely resembled stereotypes of both the Jew and the cannibal. It is also a description of the alien other that was typical of the time.

**GLOSSARY**

**D.V.**  God willing

**portmanteau**  clothes-hanger

**hypochondria**  anxiety or depression

**'events … mine'**  Romans 8:28

**'wilderness … like a rose'**  Isaiah 35:1

**blonde**  silk lace

**"with a sullen moaning sound"**  Scott, *The Lay of the Last Minstrel*, I.13.1

**Vampyre**  (German spelling) vampire

 **QUESTION**

Jane sleeps with Adèle at a turning point in her life, as she once did with Helen Burns, to what extent can Adèle therefore be seen as Jane's double?

## GLOSSARY

**a Creole** a person of European parentage born in the West Indies, Central America, tropical South America, or the Mexican Gulf; or their descendants

**'quenchless fire and deathless worm'** imagery taken from Mark 9:43–8 and Matthew 5:29

**ragout** a mixture

**'with what … judged'** Matthew 7:2

**'Funchal correspondent of his house'** representative of the Mason firm in Funchal, capital city of Madeira

**'decline'** consumption

**a subtle … Egypt** Exodus 12:23–30

**'Be not far … help'** Psalms 22:11

**'the waters … overflowed me'** Psalms 69:2

## CHAPTER 11

- Jane discovers that Rochester is already married.

Jane dresses for church and Rochester hurries her on to the ceremony. The service begins, but as the clergyman asks if there is any impediment a man steps forward to declare that Rochester is already married, to one Bertha Antoinette Mason. The stranger is a solicitor and he is accompanied by Mr Mason, Mrs Rochester's brother. Rochester admits that he has attempted bigamy and takes the church party into the house where they can meet his wife. Bertha is revealed to be a madwoman kept under lock and key, under the care of Grace Poole. Mr Mason intervened because of Jane's letter to her uncle, Mason's employee. Jane retreats to her room.

## COMMENTARY

It is worth remembering here that the Anglican marriage service had by this point become part of the state bureaucracy, a bureaucracy that extended across the Empire. Though the working classes continued to practice alternatives to legal marriage, illegitimate children were increasingly ostracised, and as a middle class woman Jane could not afford to risk her respectability as, having no property, it was the only way in which she could guarantee herself a livelihood. It was vital that she remained a virgin until her wedding day, as her whole future, not just her moral standing, would rest upon a successful marriage – which in part explains Jane's rather stand-offish behaviour since engagement. As the woman became her husband's chattel on marriage and risked her reputation, bigamy was also taken very seriously. This is why a solicitor, not simply her uncle who discovered the obstacle, comes to Jane's rescue with the declaration that 'The marriage cannot go on: I declare the existence of an impediment' (p. 323). Marriage was a matter of legal record and, for the elite in particular, was grounded in property relations.

The bad omens of the last few chapters are fulfilled. Thornfield and its master's mysteries are revealed. This is the last chapter of Volume II and serves to tie up several loose ends. We are left wondering what Jane will do next.

# VOLUME III

## CHAPTER 1

- Jane leaves Thornfield.

Next morning Jane's conscience tells her that she must leave her master. She is able to forgive Rochester, but though he tells Jane Bertha Mason's history she still refuses to become his mistress. That night Jane slips out, wanders over the fields and finally catches a coach that will take her away from the hall.

## COMMENTARY

The chapter of heightened emotion is the last in the Thornfield section and repays close analysis. It opens with an example of **personification** in which Jane looks to her Lowood training and follows 'conscience' not 'passion' (p. 335). Notice how, feeling alone and unloved as she did in childhood, she recalls the red-room at Gateshead. Her tolerance *in extremis* she draws on her schooling to provide her with inner strength.

The motif of fire and ice is repeated when Rochester takes Jane to a fire in the library to revive her. Her 'white cheek' contrasts with the 'hot rain of tears' (p. 336) that Rochester expected and are a sign of the extent to which she has controlled her passions, though at some cost – she 'had become icy cold' (p. 337). And, though she melts towards him and forgives him, she realises that she 'must be ice and rock to him' (p. 338)

The bulk of the chapter consists of Rochester's narrative, through
which we learn more about his character, how he has matured and
his current state of mind. In contrast, the brief, journalistic style in
which Jane's mental ordeal is described is striking. Symbolically the
moon is an important motif, while the dawn chorus that greets Jane
as she leaves Thornfield reminds us of her reflections on the old
chestnut tree in the hall's grounds.

Brontë once again addresses the reader directly at a time of crisis
'Reader! - I forgave him ...' (p. 336) this in a way that **foreshadows**
the style of her 'Reader, I married him' in the final chapter of
Volume III (p. 498).

Fearndean Manor is introduced as 'even more retired and hidden
than' Thornfield, in an unhealthy situation 'in the heart of a wood'
with 'damp walls' (p. 338), though later it becomes Jane and
Rochester's happy home.

Rochester describes his experiences with Bertha in tones that echo
Jane's understanding of how he would have changed her in Volume
III, Chapter 5. It is suggested that Bertha's sexual excess caused her
madness, which implies that her lunacy might have been caused by
the final stages of syphilis rather than direct inheritance.

Rochester's search for 'the antipodes of the Creole' (p. 349) is vain
in part because he seeks mistresses, in other words fallen women
who for the Victorians could only ever be likened to Magdalenes.
Though she is his wife, in allowing her sexuality to reign unchecked
this is what Bertha Mason has also become, she has prostituted
herself. And, though Jane seems to be the opposite of Bertha, this is
what she will become if she falls into the same trap, i.e. becomes
Rochester's mistress – indeed, even if she had married him, the same
fate would have befallen her as an illegitimate wife.

## CHAPTER 2

- Jane is taken in by the Rivers family.

The coach leaves Jane at Whitcross, a crossroads in the middle of the moors. She sleeps in a secluded spot and the next day sets out to look for work. She has no luck and is forced to beg. She sleeps in a wood and the next day again fails to find work.

Finally, Jane walks back into the moors and discovers an isolated farmhouse. She sees an old woman, Hannah, and two young ladies, Diana and Mary, knitting and reading in the kitchen. Jane knocks but the servant refuses to help her, but just as the door is shut in her face the master, Mr St John Rivers, returns and takes her in. When asked her name she says she is 'Jane Elliott' (p. 377).

## COMMENTARY

Jane's nature will not allow her to accept her fate passively. This chapter is full of **pathos**. The language is direct, unsentimental, and gives a very clear sense of the utter psychological and physical desolation that Jane feels at this point. This is made more poignant by the scene of perfect domesticity that greets her in her last desperate moments.

Her experiences at night on the moor, where she recognises her God's 'omnipotence' (p. 364) and 'omnipresence' is reminiscent of **Romantic** thought about Nature's ability to teach morality, as for example in Wordsworth's *The Prelude*.

Jane is, as she reflects 'brought face to face with Necessity' (p. 366). This chapter makes it clear how desperate Jane's situation is as a woman without property or family and now no prospect of a man to support her. The sexual politics are reinforced by the economic; it becomes clear that unless she, as a woman, can become *something* for someone else – a dressmaker or a servant perhaps – then she must be *nothing*, and have, as she observes, 'no claim to ask – no right to expect interest in my isolated lot' (p. 367). As such she will

**GLOSSARY**

'my Maker ... of me' Luke 12:20

'Da trat hervor ... Grimms' quotations from Schiller, *The Robbers*, V.1

'the anchor of hope ... gone' draws on Hebrews 6:19

'If I were a masterless ... tonight' Shakespeare, *King Lear* IV. 7. 35–7 remain destitute and at risk of losing her character, the only saleable commodity she really has. Unable to determine her own identity, at this point, others begin conjuring up new identities for her – by the time she is finally taken in she has already been suspected of being a beggar and a criminal. In the end, though, guided by providence, she becomes an object of charity, the best outcome that she could hope for. At which point – i.e. having become something once more – she takes back control of character and story; 'I began' she observes 'once more to know myself' (p. 378).

# CHAPTER 3

- Jane recovers.

Jane lies ill for three days but gradually recovers. When she gets up she helps the servant, Hannah, and finds out more about the Rivers family. Old Mr Rivers has just died and St John, Mary and Diana have come home to sort out his affairs. The young ladies have been working as governesses, while St John is the clergyman of the hamlet, Morton, where Jane went begging. When the family return from a walk they quiz Jane about her circumstances and history. She refuses to tell them much, but does explain that she was mostly recently a governess. She asks to be called Jane Elliott, but admits that it is not her real name. They agree to let her stay with them until she can find some kind of employment.

When Jane rises she begins a new phase of her life. From the conversation she overhears we can see how important appearance – including the quality of one's clothing and speech – was to the Victorians in helping distinguish between who was respectable and who was not. 'Respectability' was grounded in class, as well as a person's moral conduct. The two sisters also discuss Jane's 'physiognomy' (p. 380).

## COMMENTARY

This is a discreetly **expository** chapter in which we begin to learn something about the Rivers family. The two sisters and their brother are shown to be the mirror images of the Reeds, they can also be read as versions of Charlotte Brontë's own family. Jane's inherent snobbery is revealed in her conversation with Hannah, the servant, whose English Jane involuntarily corrects.

Brontë is critical of religion which exists only in the mind 'if you are a Christian, you ought not to consider poverty a crime' (p. 383). However, Jane understands and insists that the Rivers' treatment of her is 'hospitality' (p. 380) – there is a further discussion of this at the end of the chapter when St John contemplates her long-term prospects. He too is 'quite sensible of the distinction' between hospitality and '*charity*' (p. 389). Such a distinction was grounded in the material relations of rich and poor; there was a class relationship implicit in the acts of giving and receiving. Jane's refusal to see the Rivers' help as 'charity' is indicative of her sense of independence, her need to maintain her self-respect, her sense of pride, and her class identity.

### CHAPTER 4

- Jane lives happily with the Rivers and regains her health.

Jane is very happy living with the Rivers sisters who coincide with her exactly in their tastes, conversation and interests. St John remains a remote figure, but he eventually asks her to become schoolmistress at Morton. She accepts, even though she will only teach the local cottage girls, as it will allow her to become independent. She also learns that the Rivers' uncle has just died and, due to a quarrel with their father, has left them out of his will. Shortly after this the family go their separate ways.

**CHECK THE BOOK**

For a history of the concept of charity see R. Williams *Keywords: A Vocabulary of Culture and Society* (1983).

**GLOSSARY**

**enthusiasm** fanaticism

**nervous** tense and energetic

**election** individual salvation

**peace ... understanding** Philippians 4:7

eligible desirable

**church militant** role of church as the conquest of evil

**'Rise, follow me!'** see the Gospels

**ideal** imaginative, opposite of material

**cyphering** arithmetic

**'my nature ... useless'** Milton, 'When I consider ...'

**QUESTION**

Compare and contrast the characterisation of St John Rivers with that of Rochester?

## COMMENTARY

Though St John Rivers is an Evangelical clergyman he is shown to be the moral opposite of Mr Brocklehurst. Equally, compared to Rochester, St John is hard, cold, and absolutely self-controlled. St John is quite a frightening character who can clearly overpower Jane. He is so reserved that she cannot tell at first whether his dedication to the work of visiting the poor is done out of 'love or duty' (p. 393), but she later can step back and criticise his want of human affection, which is something she craves. And it soon becomes clear that his religion is grounded in labour without respite. Despite his philanthropic endeavours, he seems to lack sympathy for other human creatures and often lapses into reverie. St John's long-term intention, to become a missionary, is hinted at when he says of his work with the poor 'if I let a gust of wind … turn me away from these easy tasks, what preparation would such sloth be for the future I propose to myself?' (p. 393). And, it is quite telling that, in speaking of himself in the third person as the last male representative of the Rivers, he 'considers himself an alien from his native country – not only in life, but in death' (p. 395). This is because he looks forward to the resurrection – but this is, as with Helen Burns, a death-willing faith. And, even in his most passionate moments, when speaking of his faith, his cheek is 'unflushed' (p. 396). However, he is clearly displeased at the news that their uncle has left he and his sisters nothing in his will, ostensibly because he would have used it in doing good deeds. Jane appears uncomfortable while he discusses her new post, as he takes his time and judges her character – she dislikes the loss of control.

**GLOSSARY**

**The air … balm** Walter Scott, *The Lay of the Last Minstrel* III.14.3–4

**Lot's wife** Genesis 19:26

**Peri** beautiful good fairy

## CHAPTER 5

- Jane becomes a schoolmistress.

Jane takes up her position as schoolmistress. As she sits in her cottage on the first evening she reflects on her actions in leaving Rochester and feels that she was right to leave him, but nonetheless is very sad. St John visits her and explains that he hopes to become a missionary. While they talk a young lady, Miss Rosamond Oliver, the school's benefactress, arrives. There is an obvious mutual attraction between her and St John, though St John is careful not to show any expression of it.

## COMMENTARY

The parallels between St John and Brocklehurst continue; both men would hope to 'turn the bent of nature' (p. 404). Miss Oliver and St John are, physically, perfectly matched, like Rochester and Jane. However, St John, unlike Rochester, seems determined to turn away from love and, like Helen Burns, sacrifice himself to a death-dealing faith. Indeed, images of death often surround him. As his sister says, and Jane concurs, St John is 'inexorable as death' (p. 408). This prefigures his death at the end of the novel.

Jane struggles with her innate prejudices to see her scholars as having as much potential to learn as their social superiors. She continues to focus on her Lowood education as her beacon for good behaviour. It is quite clear to her that she might have become as Bertha did if she had followed her passions. As she looks at the harvest sunset, it is clear that she has reaped and she has sown.

> **CONTEXT**
>
> This is a typical charity school, set up with the intention of helping the poor by a local benefactress who maintains an interest in it and its pupils progress.

## CHAPTER 6

- St John steals a piece of paper.

Jane settles in at the school and becomes well liked locally, but still tends to have disturbing dreams. Miss Oliver often visits the school, when St John is teaching, and goes to the cottage when Jane is at home. Jane meets Mr Oliver and is invited to the hall where he tells her more about the Rivers family. Jane sketches Rosamond and St John appears one evening while she is working on the picture. Jane takes the opportunity to find out how he feels about Miss Oliver. As he leaves he tears and takes away a small strip of paper.

> **? QUESTION**
>
> To what extent does the representation of female desire in *Jane Eyre* challenge mid-nineteenth-century notions of morality and femininity?

Chapter 6 continued

**GLOSSARY**

**sitting in sunshine …
sweet'** Thomas
Moore, *Lalla Rookh*,
Third Day

**taken an amiable
caprice** taken a liking

*lusus naturae* (Latin)
freak of nature

**a new publication**
though Brontë says this
is Scott's *Marmion*
(1808), this does not
agree with any of the
other references to the
date at which the novel
is set (generally
1820–30s)

**'burst' … 'the silent
sea'** Coleridge, The
*Rime of the Ancient
Mariner* ll. 101–2

**'blood-bleached
robe'** Revelation 7:14

**deistic** accepts that
God exists

**'till this mortal …
immortality'** I
Corinthians 15:53

**'Cui bono'** (Latin) for
whose sake?

**GLOSSARY**

**Medusa** mythological
(female) creature with
snake hair, to look on
her is to turn to stone –
she is only defeated
when her opponent
shows her a mirror so
she gazes at her own
reflection and is turned
to stone

## COMMENTARY

Jane's dreams provide us with a very real picture of female desire
and are notable for their psychological truth. Despite her apparent
self-control, Jane is still struggling with her palpable need for
Rochester. The references to Rochester in the Morton section of the
novel serve to link this with the Thornfield chapters and help point
up the contrast between her two suitors.

St John is, as he says, 'a cold, hard, ambitious man' (p. 419),
determined to reject life in order to build 'a mansion in heaven' (p.
417). Jane cannot understand this, but, as with Helen Burns, she can
admire him and like Helen he lives a life of 'Christian stoicism' (p.
411). If Rochester is all feeling, St John is all reason. He shows
passion when Miss Oliver is near – 'his hands would tremble and
his eye burn' (p. 411) – but he resists and represses his desire. He is
a 'martyr' in that he sacrifices his feelings, and seems determined to
sacrifice himself for 'Paradise' (p. 411). Jane is right, in the long run
he does wither and waste 'under a tropical sun' (p. 416).

Jane's deception in choosing an alias is discovered, like Guy Fawkes'
plot, on 5th November. Her brief reflections on the state of modern
literature take us briefly out of the Morton episode to the narrator's
present, and suggest a degree of approbation on the part of the
actual author: *Marmion* was published in 1808, which gives us the
setting of the novel. Jane acts devilishly in tempting St John with the
painting of Miss Oliver – and then 'the original' (p. 416) i.e. Miss
Oliver herself. But St John resists her, as she will resist him.

## CHAPTER 7

• Jane inherits a fortune and gains a family.

When St John suddenly appears the next night it is to bring Jane
news. He recounts her own story and tells her that the slip of paper

he took the day before confirmed her as one 'Jane Eyre' whose uncle has died and left her £20,000. She also discovers that this man is the uncle who refused to leave a penny to the Rivers family. Jane is an heiress and has a family. She decides to divide the fortune among them all.

## COMMENTARY

Finally, Jane's fairytale begins to come true. This is one of the most deliberately fantastical elements in the story, as highlighted by the fact that it takes place at Christmas, but each piece of the puzzle has been subtly introduced earlier in the novel. Jane, still following her Lowood schooling, takes the 'Legacy' quite seriously as a responsibility to be managed.

Jane has become a woman of substance through the letter of the law, even though bequests and deeds normally benefit men – indeed, she can only benefit directly and chose how to dispose of her new-found wealth because she is not married. This acquisition coupled with Rochester's loss of property helps balance the material scales of class and of power in such a way as to permit their union, and the story begins to move to its conclusion from this point. As yet, however, Jane still entertains no thought of marriage.

Jane has longed for a real home and family since the outset of the novel. Her real identity is revealed through her art. She has also often frequently wished to have status and to be independent, see for example, Volume II, Chapter 9. The uncle in Madeira was introduced when she returned to Gateshead, in Volume II, Chapter 6, while the difficult relationships between the Rivers, Eyres and Reeds have been hinted at throughout. Images of coldness – sexual repression – versus hotness – sexual passion – are used to contrast Jane and St John's characters.

**QUESTION**

What does this action reveal about Jane, has she changed since her girlhood?

**QUESTION**

Given the fairy-tale aspect of the plotting, to what extent is the whole 'Rivers' episode convincing?

## CHAPTER 8

- St John proposes.

Jane shuts up the school for Christmas and goes back to Moor House where she and Hannah spruce the place up. Diana and Mary return to enjoy the holiday. St John tells them that he is determined to leave England and that Miss Oliver is to marry a Mr Granby. Jane is, as she hoped, treated like a sister by Diana and Mary, but St John remains reserved. He insists that she travel to the school in all weathers, and asks her to learn Hindustani. One night he kisses her on the cheek.

## COMMENTARY

Jane wants to know what has become of Rochester and writes two letters to Mrs Fairfax, but as both remain unanswered her hopes die. In the summer, St John proposes; he wants a missionary's wife and thinks that Jane will be perfect. She refuses to marry him, though she says she would accompany him to India as his sister. He will not accept this offer and they argue. After they finally shake hands, they part coolly.

While proposing St John Rivers refers to 'an East Indiaman which sails on the twentieth of June' (p. 447). Merchants who were given sole trading rights in the East Indies founded the East India Company in 1600. Their ships first arrived in India in 1608. In the 1750s the company became a ruling, not just trading, enterprise. However, soon after this the British government had to step in to bail the company out, and a Governor-General of India was put in place via the Regulation Act of 1773. British territorial expansion then proceeded with ruthless efficiency. The East India Company was dissolved in 1858.

Jane finally has a real home to return to, something she puzzled over in Volume II, Chapter 7, but she cannot imagine St John succumbing to domesticity and she shrinks in horror at the idea of being his wife. References to his being like stone associate him with Brocklehurst – though St John is clearly less hypocritical, he remains cold and hard. The long struggle – reflected in the length of the chapter – that now begins to take place between them is what finally brings her to maturity.

Jane's admiration for St John is always tempered by bleakness. She sees through his high-minded ideals, but despite this he slowly begins to overwhelm her. Her passionate nature is gradually frozen over by his kisses – the colour white clings to him as indicator of his frigidity – and her subsequent observation in the next chapter that his love would kill her seems absolutely true.

## CHAPTER 9

- St John repeats his proposal, but Jane hears Rochester calling to her.

St John continues to treat Jane coolly and refuses to respond to her overtures of friendship. They fight again and when he leaves the house she explains what is going on to Diana. That evening, after prayers, he proposes again and she nearly succumbs. Once more *in extremis* she begs God for help and suddenly hears Rochester's voice calling out to her.

## COMMENTARY

The application of principle is shown to be worse than malice and this radical departure from the conventions of nineteenth-century literature led to widespread criticism of the novel when it was first published. Here we see an admixture of the real and the fantastic as the chapter moves from the psychological to the clairvoyant – corresponding to Rochester's own experience (see next chapter). However, we discover later that her hearing Rochester's voice call to her follows his recognition of 'the hand of God' (Vol. III, Ch. 11, p. 495) in his fate. It is only after this, and once Jane recognises that her love for Rochester temporarily blinded her to God's love, that the two can be reconciled.

Jane sees through St John to 'the corrupt man within him' (p. 457). He is absolutely brutal in the execution of his faith and like Brocklehurst he is determined to bend Jane to his will, to kill her

**CONTEXT**

British soldiers and administrators needed to conduct business in Indian languages, and as they would often have to learn local vernaculars, they would generally seek the aid of a *munshi* or language instructor once they arrived.

**GLOSSARY**

'the duty of man … times' Matthew 18:21–2

'become a castaway' I Corinthians 9:27

'God sees not as man sees' I Samuel 16:7

a brand snatched from the burning Amos 4:11, Zechariah 3:2

'bid to work … shall work' John 9:4

'the fate of Dives … life' Luke 16:19–31

'that better part … from you' Luke 10:42

'rolled together like a scroll' Isaiah 34:4

true self. Where Brocklehurst was a black pillar, St John is ice-cold white marble.

The sheer power of St John's personality is quite terrifying and Jane's ultimate struggle with him is just as dramatic as her battle with Rochester in Volume III, Chapter 1. As she says 'I was almost as hard beset by him now as I had been once before, in a different way, by another' (p. 465). But, whereas she venerates St John's 'talent and principle' (p. 459), and recognises that he, like Helen, is probably one of the elect, her feelings for Rochester were much stronger – Rochester eclipsed her world, even her God. Therefore, to 'have yielded then [to Rochester] would have been an error of principle; to have yielded now [to St John] would have been an error of judgement' (p. 465).

St John and Rochester symbolise the conflict between Reason and Feeling in Jane's character. Suddenly, she transcends this conflict, realises that to be herself, in order to live, she must follow her nature 'It was *my* time to assume ascendancy. *My* powers were in play and in force' (p. 467).

**GLOSSARY**

'watch and pray ...
weak' Matthew
36:41, Mark 14:38

like the earthquake
... aghast Acts
16:26–9

tideless sea of the
south Mediterranean

## CHAPTER 10

- Jane returns to Thornfield.

The next day Jane catches the coach to Thornfield and sets out for the hall across the fields. When she reaches it she sees nothing but a shell. On asking at 'The Rochester Arms' she discovers that there has been a fire, that Bertha is dead and that Mr Rochester is alive but was maimed when he tried to save her. He is now living at Ferndean and Jane organises a carriage to take her there.

## COMMENTARY

As we reach the **denouement** so the tension mounts. Jane's departure from Morton echoes her flight from Thornfield a year earlier; but now she is absolutely sure of herself and her actions, though she has no way of guessing the consequences. She has become a mature woman who knows her own mind and can resist convention.

Jane also has the money to complete two, not just one, journeys to destinations of her choosing. And she is quite conscious of this: on stepping into the coach at Whitcross, she reflects 'I entered – not now obliged to part with my whole fortune as the price of its accommodation' (p. 470). In Volume III, Chapter 11 she makes the point that she dismisses 'the chaise and driver with the double remuneration I had promised' (p. 478). The material conditions that impact upon Jane's situation – inherent in the sexual politics of the day – remain as explicit as the ideological throughout the novel.

Her dream, in Volume II, Chapter 10, foretold that the hall would be burnt down. But it is especially shocking to her as we are reminded how closely she associates the place with the figure of its, and her, 'master' in the observation that the landscape around Thornfield 'met my eye like the lineaments of a once familiar face' (p. 470). In looking at Thornfield Hall itself, she then uses the analogy of a lover anticipating gazing upon the face of 'his mistress' (p. 472) as she sleeps only to find her lying dead. Later, of course, we find that Rochester like Thornfield has been scarred by fire. Further links to previous chapters include the fact that it burned down 'just about harvest time' (p. 473) a time when in Volume III, Chapter 5 Jane had been gazing out across the fields from her new cottage home and struggling with regret.

There's a nice observation from the old butler, in reporting the tale of the hall, that the servants 'used to watch him – servants will, you know' (p. 474). This being how she herself construed much of her own narrative – and on hearing it retold in part by the old man Jane grows, as ever when the story moves beyond her control, a little testy.

Rochester's withdrawal to Ferndean and the happy life they end up leading there is a little odd given what he says about it in Volume III, Chapter 1 and Jane's subsequent description of it, which confirms what he has said.

**QUESTION**

Why might it be necessary for Rochester to be maimed before he and Jane can finally be united?

## CHAPTER 11

- Jane arrives at Ferndean.

Jane reaches Ferndean as night falls and sees Rochester in the yard. She goes in and introduces herself to John and Mary, the servants, then takes Rochester candles and a glass of water, pretending to be the maid. Their reunion is emotional and joyful. They eat supper together and the next morning she explains what she has been doing. Eventually he proposes for the second time and she accepts.

## COMMENTARY

This is a magical chapter in which Jane and Rochester slip easily into their old ways – she teases him for a while to make him jealous then soothes him again – but in which they are both altered. Jane and Rochester have both matured; Rochester has learnt to respect Jane – his realisation at their initial meeting that 'I must be aided, and by that hand' (p. 351) comes true – while she has learnt to serve, but also to act according to her nature.

Rochester's loss of property and his injuries have in a sense 'feminised' him. It is this, aside from the convenience of losing his first wife who had been the literal legal impediment to his and Jane's marriage, that facilitates their coming together. With this and the fact that Jane has risen in the world, via a (normally masculine) stroke of luck, their relative social positions, and their gendered positions, have balanced out. This facilitates an equal companionship.

There is a little exposition at the beginning of the chapter as Fearndean manor is introduced 'a building of considerable antiquity, moderate size, and no architectural pretensions, deep buried in a wood' (p. 478). But, the language is fluid, the conversation natural.

Once inside the bounds of Fearndean, its surrounding trees effectively entrap Jane – it is dusk and she is entering a strange 'sylvan' world, slightly **Gothic** – echoing Thornfield – like that of the woodland in Shakespeare's *A Midsummer Night's Dream*. The lack of a feminine influence is suggested by the fact that there are 'no flowers, no garden-beds' (p. 479). The trees, the path, the railing, the gravel walk enclosed ground and portal, together make up a processional of privacy that she only gradually accesses. The repelling architecture of the building – its front-facing 'pointed gables', its 'narrow' 'latticed' windows and 'narrow' door (p. 479) – reflects the newly inward-looking and defensive character of its master.

We learn that Rochester called to Jane, and when she cried out in return he heard her. Rochester has learned to put his fate in God's hands and this has facilitated their union.

## CHAPTER 12

• Jane marries Rochester.

'Reader, I married him' (p. 498): Jane and Rochester marry quietly. She writes to Mary, Diana and St John; later, Diana and Mary marry. She visits Adèle and moves her from one school to another; over time the girl grows up into a pleasant young lady. Jane and Rochester are very happy together; his sight partially recovers and they have a son. St John Rivers never marries; at the close of the novel he is waiting to die in India.

## COMMENTARY

In this final chapter various loose ends are tied up. The narrator tells us what has happened to each of the key characters and links are made back across the novel – for instance we learn that Adèle has been sent to school, but that this, much like Lowood perhaps, is too strict, so Jane finds her another. Jane's prejudices – or rather those of her class and time – can be seen again in her comment that Adèle's 'sound English education corrected in a great measure her French defects' (p. 500).

**GLOSSARY**

'who live without God ... things' Philippians 3:19

bone of ... flesh Genesis 2:23

Greatheart character from Bunyan's The Pilgrim's Progress, who escorts women and children

'without fault ... God' Revelation 14:5

'incorruptible crown' I Corinthians 9:25

'good and faithful servant' Matthew 25:21

'His own words ... this' Revelation 22:20

**CONTEXT**

'Reader, I married him' is probably the most famous line in the novel.

Rochester and Jane have established a relationship based on mutual dependence. However, it is worth noting that Jane says 'Reader, I married him', not 'we were married'. It is only after Jane's powers have been established for some time that Rochester begins to regain his sight. Also, the novel does not end with Jane's description of her married bliss, but with St John's imminent death.

If we read the novel as a love story then this ending might surprise us, but if we read it as a text that deals primarily with issues of religion and sensibility, or even simply as a *Bildüngsroman*, then Jane's reflective tone becomes easier to understand. She has become a complex person; sincere yet able to question Christian doctrine, an individual who is aware of the impact of her actions on others, energetic, contemplative and self-determined, ruled in equal measure by reason and passion.

## EXTENDED COMMENTARIES

### TEXT 1 THE RED ROOM (VOL. I, CH. 2, pp. 20–2)

The red-room was a spare chamber, very seldom slept in; I might say never, indeed; unless when a chance influx of visitors at Gateshead Hall rendered it necessary to turn to account all the accommodation it contained yet it was one of the largest and stateliest chambers in the mansion. A bed supported on massive pillars of mahogany, hung with curtains of deep-red damask, stood out like a tabernacle in the centre; the two large windows, with their blinds always drawn down, were half shrouded in festoons and falls of similar drapery; the carpet was red; the table at the foot of the bed was covered with a crimson cloth; the walls were a soft fawn colour, with a blush of pink in it; the wardrobe, the toilet-table, the chairs were of a darkly polished old mahogany. Out of these deep surrounding shades rose high, and glared white, the piled-up mattresses and pillows of the bed, spread with a snowy Marseilles counterpane. Scarcely less prominent was an ample, cushioned easy-chair near the head of the bed, also white, with a footstool before it; and looking, as I thought, like a pale throne.

This room was chill, because it seldom had a fire; it was silent, because remote from the nursery and kitchens; solemn, because it was known to be so seldom entered. The house-maid alone came here on Saturdays, to wipe from the mirrors and the furniture a week's quiet dust and Mrs Reed herself, at far intervals, visited it to review the contents of a certain secret drawer in the wardrobe, where were stored divers parchments, her jewel-casket, and a miniature of her deceased husband; and in those last words lies the secret of the red-room the spell which kept it so lonely in spite of its grandeur.

Mr Reed had been dead nine years it was in this chamber he breathed his last; here he lay in state; hence his coffin was borne by the undertaker's men; and, since that day, a sense of dreary consecration had guarded it from frequent intrusion.

My seat, to which Bessie and the bitter Miss Abbot had left me riveted, was a low ottoman near the marble chimney-piece; the bed rose before me; to my right hand there was the high, dark wardrobe, with subdued, broken reflections varying the gloss of its panels; to my left were the muffled windows; a great looking-glass between them repeated the vacant majesty of the bed and room. I was not quite sure whether they had locked the door; and, when I dared move, I got up, and went to see. Alas! Yes no jail was ever more secure. Returning, I had to cross before the looking-glass; my fascinated glance involuntarily explored the depth it revealed. All looked colder and darker in that visionary hollow than in reality and the strange little figure there gazing at me, with a white face and arms specking the gloom, and glittering eyes of fear moving where all else was still, had the effect of a real spirit I thought it like one of the tiny phantoms, half fairy, half imp, Bessie's evening stories represented as coming out of lone, ferny dells in moors, and appearing before the eyes of belated travellers. I returned to my stool.

Superstition was with me at that moment; but it was not yet her hour for complete victory my blood was still warm; the mood of the revolted slave was still bracing me with its bitter vigour; I had to stem a rapid rush of retrospective thought before I quailed to the dismal present.

> **CONTEXT**
>
> Jane's superstition suggests a metaphysical philosophy. In other words, Jane's worldview includes the immaterial, the abstract; she believes that there is something beyond or independent of the human.

This passage comes from early on in *Jane Eyre*. While reading, Jane is disturbed by her cousin John Reed who picks on and throws her book at her. When she retaliates, his sisters call her aunt, Mrs Reed, who locks her in the red-room as punishment. Shortly after this passage ends, Jane loses some of her rebellious fire, becomes frightened and screams. Her aunt leaves her in the room for a further hour, by which time Jane's nerves have collapsed. The servants' apothecary is called in and, after talking with Jane, suggests that she be sent away to boarding school. Jane is an orphan and is being cared for by the Reeds because the late Mr Reed took her in and made Mrs Reed promise him that Jane would continue to live with the family after his death. Mr Reed was Jane's mother's brother.

The Gateshead section of the novel is dominated by a sense of passion, sensuality and superstition, reflecting both Jane's age – she is just ten at this point – and the more irrational side of her character. The self-indulgent Mrs Reed dominates the house, her children are spoilt brats and Jane learns to become as headstrong as the rest of them. In the red-room she begins to discover that there is a down-side to letting her emotions get the better of her, but at this point she is still enjoying their pleasant after-glow of rebellion. Her natural unease at being in her dead uncle's room is, however, gradually being intensified by her superstition and overexcited state of mind.

The tone is initially heavy, as lugubrious as the stately furniture itself while the silence and abandonment of the room is suggested by words like 'subdued', 'muffled', 'vacant'; even the dust is 'quiet'. We see the room from Jane's nervous point of view and she sees the objects within it quite unnaturally. The bed is not simply a bed but becomes a 'tabernacle', the chair beside it becomes 'a pale throne', she herself becomes 'a real spirit', a 'tiny phantom, half fairy, half imp'. Each object metamorphoses into something that is alien and frightening and though the scene is described quite tersely, journalistically, it is also highly suggestive.

The way of seeing described in this passage stays with Jane throughout the novel. Whenever she is unable to explain an experience or other phenomenon she looks for a supernatural or unnatural origin for the marvel. As she matures and learns about it

**CONTEXT**

Eighteenth-century **Gothic** novels were usually set in the past, often in Southern European Catholic countries, and featured spectacular landscapes, castles and monasteries, as well as fantastical and eerie goings on.

in more detail, she begins to assign the emotion, experience or object a rational explanation. Shortly after this passage ends, for instance, she says that she wondered as a child why she merited such bad treatment from the Reeds; as an adult she is able to reflect on this and explain that it was because she was so unlike them. We are therefore drawn into sympathy for Jane as she sits alone and frightened in a haunted room, but we also gain a more mature understanding of the way in which she has brought much of her ill-treatment upon herself. The point at which she looks into the mirror crystallises one such moment of balanced perception.

The mirror in which she sees herself as a phantom, the punishment of sitting on a chair in a locked and abandoned room for a fit of passion, also forms a link between Jane and Mrs Rochester, who is also described as a kind of phantom. The redness of the room itself is symbolic of passion and unreason, and of course it houses secrets – the symbols of Mrs Reed's property and wealth inherited from her husband – just like the attic at Thornfield Hall. This prefigures the link that is established between Jane and Bertha when Jane wanders, daydreaming on the third storey at Thornfield – 'if there were a ghost at Thornfield, this would be its haunt' – and suggests that if she had not learnt to control her irrational instincts and had stayed with Edward Rochester, then she would have also have become, if not actually a madwoman, then as powerless and lacking in the ability to control her own life as a madwoman.

## TEXT 2 ROCHESTER'S PROPOSAL (VOL. II, CH. 8, pp. 282–5)

'Come – we'll talk over the voyage and the parting quietly, half an hour or so, while the stars enter into their shining life up in heaven yonder here is the chestnut tree; here is the bench at its old roots. Come, we will sit there in peace to-night, though we should never more be destined to sit there together.' He seated me and himself.

'It is a long way to Ireland, Janet, and I am sorry to send my little friend on such weary travels but if I can't do better, how is it to be helped? Are you anything akin to me, do you think, Jane?'

> **CONTEXT**
>
> By the nineteenth century, **Gothic** writing had become more domestic; though still suspenseful and supernatural, Gothic novels were generally given English, often urban, settings and focused on the home.

Text 2 Rochester's Proposal (Vol. II, ch. 8, pp. 282–5) continued

I could risk no sort of answer by this time my heart was full.

'Because,' he said, 'I sometimes have a queer feeling with regard to you – especially when you are near me, as now it is as if I had a string somewhere under my left ribs, tightly and inextricably knotted to a similar string situated in the corresponding quarter of your little frame. And if that boisterous channel, and two hundred miles or so of land come broad between us, I am afraid that cord of communion will be snapt; and then I've a nervous notion I should take to bleeding inwardly. As for you, – you'd forget me.'

'That I *never* should, sir you know –' impossible to proceed.

'Jane, do you hear that nightingale singing in the wood? Listen!'

In listening, I sobbed convulsively; for I could repress what I endured no longer; I was obliged to yield, and I was shaken from head to foot with acute distress. When I did speak, it was only to express an impetuous wish that I had never been born, or never come to Thornfield.

'Because you are sorry to leave it?'

The vehemence of emotion, stirred by grief and love within me, was claiming mastery, and struggling for full sway; and asserting a right to predominate to overcome, to live, rise, and reign at last; yes, – and to speak.

'I grieve to leave Thornfield I love Thornfield – I love it, because I have lived in it a full and delightful life, – momentarily at least. I have not been trampled upon. I have not been petrified. I have not been buried with inferior minds, and excluded from every glimpse of communion with what is bright and energetic, and high. I have talked, face to face, with what I reverence; with what I delight in, – with an original, a vigorous, an expanded mind. I have known you, Mr Rochester; and it strikes me with terror and anguish to feel I absolutely must be torn from you for ever. I see the necessity of departure; and it is like looking on the necessity of death.'

'Where do you see the necessity?' he asked, suddenly.

**CHECK THE FILM**

To help you visualise and think about Jane's plainness relative to the splendour and good looks of her superiors, watch Franco Zeffirelli's 1996 adaptation. This production stars William Hurt, Charlotte Gainsbourg, Joan Plowright, Anna Paquin and Elle MacPherson and remains close to the novel's original characterisation, but do go back to the text for the detail.

'Where? You, sir, have placed it before me.'

'In what shape?'

'In the shape of Miss Ingram; a noble and beautiful woman, – your bride.'

'My bride! What bride? I have no bride!'

'But you will have.'

'Yes; – I will! I will!' He set his teeth.

'Then I must go – you have said it yourself.'

'No you must stay! I swear it – and the oath shall be kept.'

'I tell you I must go!' I retorted, roused to something like passion. 'Do you think I can stay to become nothing to you? Do you think I am an automaton? – a machine without feelings? and can bear to have my morsel of bread snatched from my lips, and my drop of living water dashed from my cup? Do you think, because I am poor, obscure, plain, and little, I am soulless and heartless? – You think wrong! – I have as much soul as you, – and full as much heart! And if God had gifted me with some beauty, and much wealth, I should have made it as hard for you to leave me, as it is now for me to leave you. I am not talking to you now through the medium of custom, conventionalities, nor even of mortal flesh – it is my spirit that addresses your spirit; just as if both had passed through the grave, and we stood at God's feet, equal – as we are!'

'As we are! Repeated Mr Rochester – 'so,' he added, enclosing me in his arms, gathering me to his breast, pressing his lips on my lips 'so, Jane!'

'Yes, so, sir,' I rejoined 'and yet not so; for you are a married man – or as good as a married man, and wed to one inferior to you – to one with whom you have no sympathy – whom I do not believe you truly love; for I have seen and heard you sneer at her. I would scorn such a union therefore I am better than you – let me go!'

'Where, Jane? To Ireland?'

> **CONTEXT**
>
> Charlotte's father emigrated from Ireland to England as a young man.

'Yes – to Ireland. I have spoken my mind, and can go anywhere now.'

'Jane, be still; don't struggle so, like a wild, frantic bird that is rending its own plumage in its desperation.'

'I am no bird; and no net ensnares me I am a free human being with an independent will; which I now exert to leave you.'

Another effort set me at liberty, and I stood erect before him.

'And your will shall decide your destiny,' he said 'I offer you my hand, my heart, and a share of all my possessions.'

This passage comes almost midway through *Jane Eyre*. By this point Jane has left Gateshead and has since spent eight years at Lowood school, as pupil and then teacher, where she has learnt about self-sacrifice from her friend Helen Burns and self-control from her teacher Miss Temple. After advertising for a place as a governess she accepted a position at Thornfield Hall.

Jane and the master of Thornfield, Mr Edward Fairfax Rochester, have gradually become friends and, while taking some time off to visit her dying aunt, Jane has discovered that she has fallen in love with him. However, as far as she is concerned, Mr Rochester is too far above her in station for anything to come of this, and she expects him to marry a local heiress, Miss Blanche Ingram – partly because of rumours he has himself circulated to test Jane's feelings.

It is sunset on Midsummer's-eve and the garden is full of sweet scents and song, but soon after Jane accepts Rochester's proposal the chestnut tree is split in two by a violent storm. The wedding is interrupted and called off when it is suddenly revealed that Mr Rochester is already married. His wife is a madwoman kept under lock-and-key, but Jane cannot countenance his attempted bigamy and flees.

As Jane gradually moves, Eve-like, from innocence to understanding we are provided with a lyrical example of the naturalistic dialogue that regularly takes place between the two lovers. Their conversations bring the characters alive and through

**CHECK THE BOOK**

For more about gardens and their uses in nineteenth-century fiction see M. Waters *The Garden in Victorian Literature* (1988).

them Brontë makes a complete break with the novels of her time. Where other authors avoided this kind of complex exchange, by glossing over the characters' speeches or using paraphrase, and some produced only a stilted and clumsy impression of speech, Brontë manages to move rapidly and confidently between confusion, explanation, and exclamation in such a way as to allow us to understand Jane's turmoil and Rochester's own inner conflict.

Jane is quite powerless, given her social position, but speaks as an individual who demands to be treated with respect and fights to maintain her identity – 'I am no bird;… I am a free human being with an independent will' – and so talks on behalf of her sex. She does not want to be exiled, but fights for her self-respect by demanding that she be permitted to leave rather than watch Rochester enter a conventional marriage based on property. In the process she rehearses her history to date 'I have not been trampled on. I have not been petrified. I have not been buried with inferior minds'. She is trying to reconcile passion with duty, 'and it is like looking on the necessity of death'.

Rochester, half talking to Jane, half thinking out loud – 'if I can't do better, how is it to be helped?' – tests her love and is working up to asking her for her hand. The reason for his hesitation becomes clear on their wedding-day, and is unwittingly **foreshadowed** by Jane – 'you are a married man … and wed to one inferior to you' – while she still thinks he intends to marry Miss Ingram. Ironically, Miss Ingram does in fact look like and behave as his wife did before she went mad.

In loving Jane, Rochester hopes to find Bertha's antithesis – 'the antipodes of the Creole' (Vol. III, Ch. 1, p. 349). Though Jane has begun to mature and combine passion with self-control, however, Rochester has yet to learn from his experiences or face the consequences of his actions. As he pours out his love against the nightingale's song, he still needs to realise that Jane will only love him in return if he treats her with respect. Though his love is quite genuine, his proposal is essentially built on a secret and is therefore enslaving, dishonourable and shallow the Midsummer's fairytale is about to go wrong.

**CHECK THE BOOK**

For a detailed discussion of the relationship between the woman writer and her mad double – in fictional form – see S. M. Gilbert and S. Gubar *The Madwoman in the Attic the Woman Writer and the Nineteenth-Century Imagination* (1984).

**CHECK THE FILM**

Think about the extent to which Jane finds Thornfield a happy home, despite the screechings and screams she hears. In his 1996 film, Franco Zeffirelli's makes Jane's room light and pleasant, while the regions of the house controlled by Rochester are darker, more sinister.

At this point Jane and Rochester are doomed, as is soon suggested in the storm that breaks out over their heads. The chestnut tree under which Jane and Rochester sit is a symbol of life, but quickly becomes an omen of ill-fortune and they are chased out of the paradisiacal garden as Rochester asks God to sanction their marriage. The Thornfield section of the novel is often simultaneously personal and symbolic in this way. Rochester gives Thornfield Hall life and a sense of purpose when he is there, but it is also symbolically identified with him. When Jane first tours the building there are vague **foreshadowings** of what she will find out about it and its master. By the end of the novel, when he has finally learnt his lesson, Rochester likens his own maimed body to the shriven tree's black form.

## TEXT 3 ST JOHN'S PROPOSAL (VOL. III, CH. 9, pp. 465–7)

I stood motionless under my hierophant's touch. My refusals were forgotten – my fears overcome – my wrestlings paralysed. The Impossible – *i.e.* my marriage with St John – was fast becoming the Possible. All was changing utterly, with a sudden sweep. Religion called – Angels beckoned – God commanded – life rolled together like a scroll – death's gates opening, shewed eternity beyond it seemed, that for safety and bliss there, all here might be sacrificed in a second. The dim room was full of visions.

'Could you decide now?' asked the missionary. The inquiry was put in gentle tones he drew me to him as gently. Oh, that gentleness! how far more potent is it than force! I could resist St John's wrath I grew pliant as a reed under his kindness. Yet I knew all the time, if I yielded now, I should not the less be made to repent, some day, of my former rebellion. His nature was not changed by one hour of solemn prayer it was only elevated.

'I could decide if I were but certain,' I answered 'were I but convinced that it is God's will I should marry you, I could vow to marry you here and now – come afterwards what would!'

'My prayers are heard!' ejaculated St John. He pressed his hand firmer on my head, as if he claimed me he surrounded me with his arm, *almost* as if he loved me (I say *almost* – I knew the difference – for I had felt what it was to be loved; but, like him, I had now put love out of the question, and thought only of duty) I contended with my inward dimness of vision, before which clouds yet rolled. I sincerely, deeply, fervently longed to do what was right; and only that. 'Shew me, shew me the path!' I entreated of Heaven. I was excited more than I had ever been; and whether what followed was the effect of excitement, the reader will judge.

All the house was still; for I believe all, except St John and myself, were now retired to rest. The one candle was dying out the room was full of moonlight. My heart beat fast and thick I heard its throb. Suddenly it stood still to an inexpressible feeling that thrilled it through, and passed at once to my head and extremities. The feeling was not like an electric shock; but it was quite as sharp, as strange, as startling it acted on my senses as if their utmost activity hitherto had been but torpor; from which they were now summoned, and forced to wake. They rose expectant eye and ear waited, while the flesh quivered on my bones.

'What have you heard? What do you see?' asked St John. I saw nothing but I heard a voice somewhere cry –

'Jane! Jane! Jane!' nothing more.

'Oh God! What is it?' I gasped.

I might have said, 'Where is it?' for it did not seem in the room – nor in the house – nor in the garden it did not come out of the air – nor from under the earth – nor from overhead. I had heard it – where, or whence, for ever impossible to know! And it was the voice of a human being – a known, loved, well-remembered voice – that of Edward Fairfax Rochester; and it spoke in pain and woe wildly, eerily, urgently.

'I am coming!' I cried. 'Wait for me! Oh, I will come!'

The passage comes from the latter half of *Jane Eyre*. After the abortive marriage ceremony at Thornfield, Jane feels that she must leave the hall. Having used all her money and losing her possessions in her escape, she wanders destitute for several days, forced to beg

**CONTEXT**

Jane's hearing Rochester call to her after she has cried out to God implies that there is no need for the clergy mediate between Christ and his followers. This was a radical proposition at the time and fed into the religious debate about the novel.

Text 3 St John's proposal (Vol. III, ch. 9, pp. 465–7) continued

**CONTEXT**

Nineteenth-century stage adaptations tended to tame and domesticate Jane, presumably finding her too subversive – she had to be represented either as a good moral woman or as a selfish and wilful one, it was difficult for her to be seen as both virtuous and strong-minded at this time.

for help. She is turned away by everyone, until, starving and cold, St John Rivers takes her in. She and his two sisters, Mary and Diana, become friends and he offers her the post of local schoolmistress. She does not like the work but accepts the position.

During this period in her life she lives by the name Jane Elliott, but when Rivers discovers her true identity he is able to tell her that she has inherited a fortune. He knows this because they are in fact related and Jane promptly shares out the money equally between herself and the others. After this Mary and Diana treat her like a sister and St John begins to teach her Hindustani. Eventually he proposes.

St John wants her to go with him to India as a missionary's wife. She says she will go as his sister, but he will only take her if she will marry him. In this passage he presses her on the subject again, but, after hearing the mysterious voice, she determines to find out what has become of Rochester. She goes back to Thornfield and discovers that it has been destroyed by fire, its master maimed in the attempt to save his wife who has fallen to her death. She seeks out Rochester and finally they marry.

St John is as hard and 'cold as an iceberg' (Vol. III, Ch. 3, p. 386) – in opposition to Mr Brocklehurst who is 'a black pillar' (Vol. I, Ch. 4, p. 40) – but in this passage he becomes gentle in an attempt to draw Jane into his plans. The setting is eerie and faintly unnatural the room in which Jane and St John stand is dark, except for a guttering candle and the moonlight; outside all is black and silent except for the soughing March wind. It is night-time and everyone else has retired to bed. The language is journalistic and the tone of the piece is tense, thrilling, but quite unlike that of the garden scene in which Rochester proposed.

St John is utterly unable to bend himself to the yoke of mutual love and tenderness, and as such, is the opposite of Mr Rochester who helps Jane to the full enjoyment of life – as she herself recognises in parenthesis. There is no sympathy between them, St John simply tries to dominate Jane – 'He pressed his hand firmer on my head, as if he claimed me' – and, as we can see from the self-conscious stress on '*almost*', only ever gives the appearance of love. He may seem to be a high-minded clergyman, but he is actually a thug who is determined that others will submit to his will and sacrifice themselves to his cause – 'My prayers are heard!' he cries as she says she *might* marry him.

Jane has already seen through the gloss of right-minded missionary to the ambitious man within – 'I should not the less be made to repent, some day, of my former rebellion' – but she still finds it hard to withstand his assaults on her own hard-won identity. This is because she wants to do what is morally right. Through St John and Jane's relationship Brontë exposes the Victorian myth of self-denying asceticism which, juxtaposed against a real and deeply felt morality that has nothing to do with social convention, is shown to equate with the heartless sacrifice of others.

Where Rochester tempted Jane to throw away social convention and duty, so St John tempts her to throw away her passion, to renounce her nature entirely. And because fate has brought them together she finds it hard to see clearly whether or not she should marry him – 'I contended with my inward dimness of vision, before which clouds yet rolled'. However, Rochester's love is transcendent. And, as Jane cries to Heaven for help, so she receives her aid and escapes his death-willing vision of faith. Where Rochester called out to God to sanction the bigamous marriage, St John calls on God to support his own shallow and essentially meaningless proposal. Where Providence previously spoke through the destruction of the chestnut tree, this time Jane hears Rochester's voice.

**CONTEXT**

Bigamy, along with illegitimacy and adultery, became a staple plot device in the Sensation Novels of the 1860s. Sensation Novels, which like Mary Braddon's *Lady Audley's Secret* (1862) could be highly subversive, were enormously popular. They were not treated as having 'literary' merit in their day, but there was debate about their corruption of the public taste.

# PART THREE

## CRITICAL APPROACHES

 QUESTION

Consider each major character's narrative function.

# CHARACTERISATION

## JANE EYRE

Jane Eyre is essentially a young woman who is trying to grow up in a society that does not value her or her skills, and as such carries the theme of the novel. She is an advocate for her sex, and asserts herself, liberates herself and makes herself happy because she believes she has a right to be so. Jane is a credible and realistic character and it is therefore all too easy to treat her as a real person who has an independent existence beyond the text. We get to know her innermost thoughts and deepest feelings through the course of the novel; in fact the heart of the novel actually lies in Jane's descriptions of what is going on in her own mind, and we are therefore drawn into a very close relationship with her. However, Jane is also Cinderella-like, or like the heroine of 'The Beauty and the Beast', though unlike these fairytale characters Jane is plain both as a child and as an adult. As Mr Rochester's servants comment at Ferndean in the Conclusion, 'she ben't one o' th' handsomest' (Vol. III, Ch. 12, p. 499).

Jane is born poor, is soon orphaned and lives out her childhood with her Aunt Reed and three cousins who detest and bully her. Unlike Cinderella she does not have to work as a servant, but her life at Gateshead and then at Lowood school is one of drudgery. Even when she becomes a governess she is still placed in an awkward social position, because at the time governesses were a social anomaly. Neither servants nor members of their employer's family, governesses had to be respectable young ladies when respectable young ladies were not supposed to work for their living. Jane's prospects finally pick up, however, when she discovers that she has an alternative set of cousins who will treat her as an equal and when, rather than a fairy godmother, her rich uncle finally leaves her enough money to become independent. Eventually, she marries her very own handsome 'prince', Mr Rochester, and the novel ends 'My Edward and I ... are happy' (Vol. III, Ch. 12,

**CONTEXT**

The Governesses Benevolent Institution was established in 1841.

p. 501). It is, therefore, the complex psychic development that Jane undergoes and the everyday setting of the novel that manage to make her such an impressive character, rather than her somewhat implausible story.

**QUESTION**

Is *Jane Eyre* a simple fairy story?

Jane dominates and controls the narrative – incidentally, remember that a first-person narrator is not the author despite the subtitle – and her reactions and feelings always form the focus of attention, even when another character is talking about him or herself. And because we are privy to her innermost thoughts, we generally take her to be a reliable observer. But it is important to remember here that Jane is narrating events ten years after they have happened. Though she is a child at Gateshead, she tells us about this period as a mature woman, and she herself reminds us of this.

Jane is not a wholly sympathetic figure, either, for example, as we see in Volume I, Chapter 3, she is quite a precocious child. She is middle class by birth and though impoverished herself she has to learn that the poor are not just an amorphous mass. She can therefore be quite a snob. As an adult, she is also thoroughly imbued with the idea that everything foreign is intrinsically unhealthy and immoral. She makes sure that little Adèle learns to be English, or at least as English as possible, given that she is a French Catholic, and she assumes that the Indian climate will kill her. These are the attitudes of her time and of her class.

**QUESTION**

To what extent are Jane's attitudes and prejudices typical of her class?

At the beginning of the novel Jane is angry, rebellious and hungry for adventure, but as she grows up she learns how to temper her wilder passions so that, unlike many characters in Victorian novels, she is not destroyed by them. Her feelings, especially 'conscience' and 'passion' (Vol. III, Ch. 1, p. 335), are often given voices of their own when she is suffering some particular anguish and these moments of **personification** help us to understand why she acts as she does. Torn throughout the novel between her true nature and social convention, in the end she is able to resolve this inherent division by marrying for duty and for love. Yet that victory is one that only she can achieve by force of will and the sacrifice of the characters who are closest to her.

**?  QUESTION**

Consider how Mr
Rochester's and Mr
Rivers' characters
are revealed by
their actions or
speech?

## MR ROCHESTER AND ST JOHN RIVERS

Mr Rochester's growth is important to the unfolding of the plot but, as a secondary character, he is slightly less convincing than Jane Eyre. His story is one of sin and redemption and he is a **Romantic** figure who is well-bred, with brooding, rugged good looks, and combines masculine strength with tenderness. Forceful, passionate and independent, he is determined to have Jane, either as his wife or as his mistress, whatever the cost, yet he is not selfish. We do not generally know his innermost thoughts because Jane does not know them, but we learn a lot about him from his conversations with her; their witty banter brings both characters alive.

Rochester never tries to woo Jane on bended knee; he does not idealise her and she can always match him blow for blow when they argue. Rochester often refers to Jane as a bird, fairy, a sprite and an imp, and he toys with her, hoping to make her jealous, but he eventually learns that he must depend on, respect and see her as an individual if he is to win her hand. This outcome is **foreshadowed** by their first meeting, when his horse falls in the road and he has to lean on her in order to get home. In the end, his dependence on her is made absolute by his blindness, at which point she loves him more than when he simply tried to protect her or shower her with gifts.

**CONTEXT**

A legally
separated wife
could not keep her
own earnings until
the Matrimonial
Causes Act of
1857. Married
women did not
receive the same
rights over their
property –
including wages
and inheritance –
as single women
until the Married
Woman's Property
Act in 1882.

The courtship scenes present us with a remarkable departure from literary convention. Through them we see the development of mutual respect between the two major characters; Rochester and Jane's relationship is one that eventually results in a marriage of equals. As Jane says in the final chapter of the novel 'To be together is for us to be at once as free as in solitude, as gay as in company. To talk to each other is but a more animated and audible thinking' (Vol. III, Ch. 12, p. 500). However, the happy ever after is only made possible because Rochester has been clipped, tamed and chained like an eagle. His disability enables Jane to combine passion with duty. The price of Jane Eyre's happiness is therefore Edward Rochester's sight and right hand.

Rochester is not simply a realistic character, however, he is also symbolic of the part of Jane that is fiery and passionate, rather than icy and self-controlled, and as such he is St John Rivers's opposite. They look like opposites and they act as foils to each other. Rochester is heavy and dark, whereas St John is handsome and fair; Rochester is a man of passion and fire, whereas St John is ambitious, hard and cold. Where Rochester brings Jane alive, she finds St John's passion quite deadly.

St John Rivers is not a sympathetic character, unlike Rochester, but he is still fairly reliable – he is quite honest about his limitations – and convincing. St John, a strict clergyman, lives up to the principles espoused by the Evangelical school proprietor, Mr Brocklehurst; St John is 'a white stone' (Vol III, Ch. 8, p. 418) to Brocklehurst's 'black pillar' (Vol. I, Ch. 4, p. 40). St John is ruthlessly moral and therefore, unlike Brocklehurst, not a hypocrite. St John always acts consistently but unnaturally, as suggested by the fact that he will not follow his nature and marry the woman he loves; his faith, like that of Helen Burns, is one that is death-dealing and grounded in self-sacrifice.

St John therefore symbolises that side of Jane's character which wishes to conform, to obey the rules and suppress her instincts. However, Jane recognises that if she accepts him as her husband she will be crushed, she will lose her identity just as surely as if she had become Rochester's mistress. Both men represent only one half of her and this is why she runs away from St John, back to Thornfield. It is worth noting though that the final passages in the novel are devoted to St John. Like Helen Burns he is about to die in consummation of his faith and this makes Jane cry. His path has led to death, in contrast to her own which has led to life-giving happiness.

## MINOR CHARACTERS

### *Bessie*

Jane wins her first moral victory over the nursemaid Bessie who, though she is a relatively minor character, reappears several times – at Lowood and when Jane returns to Gateshead – thus providing a link between the earlier and later parts of the novel. Bessie's ballads and folklore stay with Jane throughout the text, and because Bessie

 **QUESTION**

How does Jane's relationship with Bessie change and what does this reveal about Jane herself?

is the only real figure of ordinary, unrefined human kindness in the book she is one of the most sympathetic characters we meet.

## The Reeds

The Reed family, on the other hand, are utterly detestable. They treat Jane as a nobody, and because we see them entirely from Jane's point of view it is hard to see any good in them. Mrs Reed hates Jane because she has been foisted upon them and Jane's cousins take their lead from their mother. Jane is unhappy and her aunt knows that by treating Jane so badly she is not really obeying her husband's last wish, and Jane always asserts her right to be happy, to be loved above all else. Because of this Mrs Reed feels a certain amount of guilt about Jane; she is tormented by her and this means that she must be expelled from their society. The Reeds show us how Jane is a social outcast and her response to them demonstrates how she blankly refuses to accept her lot.

## The Rivers

The Rivers family present us with a mirror image of the Reed family. Unlike the Reeds, the Rivers family offer Jane genuine help when they take her in. Where the two Reed sisters, Eliza and Georgiana, represent two extremes of femininity that are equally despicable, the two Rivers sisters, Diana and Mary, are ideal women and become Jane's role models. Where her cousin John Reed physically abused her, her cousin St John Rivers becomes her teacher.

**CONTEXT**

The River family were reputedly modelled closely on Charlotte's own sisters and brother, though in idealised form.

## Mr Brocklehurst

Just before Jane leaves Gateshead Mrs Reed introduces Jane to the proprietor of Lowood school, Mr Brocklehurst. At Lowood school Jane faces the same treatment as she received at Gateshead, but on a larger scale and in a religious community. Both Gateshead and Lowood work as models of Victorian society, but Brocklehurst in particular represents a form of religious doctrine that Jane instinctively rejects. His faith is all hell-fire and brimstone, he oppresses the children under his care with an extreme Evangelical zeal.

At one point Brocklehurst picks on a girl, Julia Severn, who has curly red hair, simply because he assumes that she must have curled it by artifice. When he is told that her curls are natural he then insists that it be cut off because the children should not conform to nature. While this is going on his own daughters are described as being dressed in fine clothes and wearing their hair according to the latest fashion. This certainly suggests that his religious principles are a mockery of Christianity, that he is a hypocrite who cannot act consistently, but it also suggests that anyone who deviates from the hypocritical standards he sets must be cut out like a canker. He is an example of the men who held power in Victorian Britain and the message is that when men like Brocklehurst hold the reins, then there is no way to live and be yourself; anyone who fails to conform will be pushed out of the way.

### Helen Burns

When Jane goes to school she is not simply subject to Brocklehurst's rule, however, she also makes friends with Helen Burns who, in sharp contrast to Brocklehurst, represents an ideal of Christian practice. Helen's initial interest in *Rasselas* tells the reader everything he or she needs to know about her. This book argues that only surrender and self-control will enable us to bear with the difficulties of life; Helen endures this world simply because she, like St John, can look forward to the joys of the next. For instance, Helen is picked on by one of the teachers, but always turns the other cheek and, as an ideal woman, meekly resigns herself to her fate.

### Miss Temple

When Helen dies of tuberculosis Jane soon rejects this apparently death-dealing vision of self-sacrifice, but quickly falls under the perfect Miss Temple's spell. Miss Temple, Jane's teacher, also has to conform. When she follows her best instincts and gives the children an extra lunch because they have missed breakfast, we are quite clear that she is in the right, but she dare not talk back to Mr Brocklehurst when he upbraids her for her simple kindness. Miss Temple's self-control is a model for Jane until her mentor leaves the school, at which point her influence begins to fade. Through her

> **CONTEXT**
>
> As a stoic Helen Burns believes that to live virtuously, a person must live in accord with nature. Many 'good' things in life, e.g. health, are often virtuous, but not always – for instance they may be acquired at the expense of integrity. To be virtuous a person must therefore maintain constant vigilance and be aware of the choices they make.

friendship with these characters Jane learns the sacrifices demanded of women and, once she is beyond their influence, quickly looks for an alternative.

## Mrs Rochester

One alternative to the ideal of Victorian femininity would be a complete rejection of self-control, as embodied by Mrs Rochester. Bertha is Jane Eyre's *alter ego*, that side of Jane that is driven entirely by passion. She is Rochester's wife, the role promised to Jane, but which she prevents Jane from taking up, as symbolised by her destruction of Jane's veil on the night before the wedding. Jane has some control over her life however, whereas Bertha as a madwoman and an outcast is powerless. A renewed adoption of the values embodied by Helen and Miss Temple therefore allows Jane to escape Bertha's fate. If Jane had followed her heart's desire and stayed with Rochester at this point, she would in a sense have become another Bertha, another madwoman driven purely by her appetites. Luckily, of course, Bertha's final act means that Jane can ultimately resolve the opposition in herself between passion and self-control.

## Miss Ingram, Miss Oliver and Mrs Fairfax

These three women, because they are simply foils for the other characters, remain relatively two-dimensional and seem in effect to be cast aside once their job is done. Miss Blanche Ingram is described as 'a real strapper … big, brown and buxom' (Vol. II, Ch. 5, p. 245) and therefore looks just like Mrs Rochester, and in many respects also behaves like her, before she married Edward. But Rochester simply uses Blanche in order to discover Jane's feelings and once he is done with the heiress we hear no more about her – we do not even know if she finally marries.

Miss Rosamond Oliver, in direct contrast to Jane, is both moneyed and beautiful. An 'earthly angel' she is the perfect match for St John Rivers who loves but spurns her simply because he knows that she would not make a good missionary's wife. This is how we come to realise with Jane that St John is indeed 'hard and cold' (Vol. III, Ch. 8, p. 438). The last we hear about Rosamond is that she 'is about

---

**CONTEXT**

Bertha is a 'Creole'. Today 'Creole' refers to a language, combining African and French languages, and to French and Spanish settlers in the southern United States especially in and around Louisiana, but then it also meant someone born of African and French, or African and Spanish, ancestry.

to be married to Mr Granby, one of the best matches and most estimable residents in S–' (Vol. III, Ch. 8, p. 440). St John sees this as a victory.

Mrs Fairfax, the housekeeper, is a distant relative of Mr Rochester's who, like Jane, is poor but genteel. Where Jane's father was a clergyman, Mrs Fairfax was married to one. She shows Jane, and therefore the reader too, around Thornfield and provides information about the locality and people, including its master. Unlike Jane, however, Mrs Fairfax is not a great observer of character and quickly takes a back seat soon after Jane meets Rochester. Mrs Fairfax then hovers in the background as a moral bystander until Jane leaves Thornfield. When Jane returns we learn that the housekeeper has been sent away to her friends with a handsome annuity.

> **CONTEXT**
>
> To become a housekeeper a woman would normally work her way up through the servant ranks, from scullery-maid onwards. She was the highest ranking female servant in the household and answered directly to the mistress, where there was one.

# THEMES

## MORAL COURAGE

The central theme of the novel is explored through one young woman's attempt to grow up and gain respect in a society that does not value her or her talents. The problem of being a woman in early Victorian Britain is the key to our understanding of the text. To begin with, at Gateshead, Jane learns that moral courage can give her the power to withstand moral oppression. Because of this she is able to make friends with Bessie and dominate her surrogate stepmother, Aunt Reed. As she enters Lowood, however, she is again exposed to injustice and encounters two new ways of dealing with this, first in the form of stoic Christian forgiveness and meekness, as embodied in Helen Burns, and secondly submission to social custom, as embodied in Miss Temple. She takes both on board for a while, but neither seems to satisfy her. She discovers that she must be true to herself and that to achieve this she must become independent.

## SEARCH FOR IDENTITY

Jane's search for identity takes her to Thornfield where she finds some happiness, but where she is still restless until the master of the house appears. After she follows her deepest desires and accepts Rochester's proposal she becomes acutely sensitive to signs of ill-fortune and is all too aware of the bad omens that surround their future marriage, but is still unprepared to deal with the consequences of her actions when the final calamity falls. When she discovers that Rochester is already married, albeit to a madwoman, she acts entirely according to convention, as learned at Lowood, by fleeing Thornfield in order to regain some self-control. She does not succumb to passion because her education has shown her that passion is not a fit motive for action. If she lived with Rochester she would be a social outcast and lose her partial and hard-won individualism.

## SELF-FULFILMENT

For a while, this seems to have been the right move. After the Rivers family rescue her, she finds all that she ever wanted, money, status, a family, a home. Hard work and a sound morality are seen to bring their own reward. However, as St John Rivers asks her to marry him simply for form's sake and become a missionary's wife, she rediscovers her true self. She finds that she cannot completely abandon her passions after all. It is only when she returns to Rochester, having matured and learnt the necessity of combining desire with duty, that she can live happily ever after. The novel is therefore about woman's intellectual and emotional needs, the search for identity, and the way in which passion has to be reconciled with self-control.

We can also see that it is not enough for a woman simply to be respectable or independent.

No matter how rewarding it is for an unmarried woman to make a success of her life through quiet perseverance and a clear moral stand, it is better if she can share her life with an equal, someone who is a companion who will support her and who is dependent on her, and of course the novel ends with a marriage of equals. Rochester's development is important here in helping Jane complete her own growth.

The events that shape the novel therefore test Jane and give the reader the opportunity to explore her deepest motivations and

**CONTEXT**

It was still being said in 1880 that the 'missionary and educational work in India China … and other parts of the world, offers a vast and most interesting field to young women of intelligence earnest religious opinions, and some enterprise, who have few home ties, and are quick at adapting themselves to new conditions of life.'

feelings. The plot, characters and language all form an exploration of the theme, but, as we have just seen, to a large extent in this instance, the theme actually dictates the form.

## SOCIAL CLASS

Another, less obvious, theme tackles the much broader problem of social class. Though on one level the novel is a love story which covers the experiences of one woman, a representative of her sex, it also deals with the difficulties faced by a particular class of women in Victorian society young middle-class women – especially governesses – who were poor. Interestingly, it does not really provide these women with a radical solution to their problems.

Though Jane makes a success of her own life, through sheer force of will coupled with a lucky inheritance, she does not offer a way out for those middle-class women who remained poor, or for those who wanted to break the bounds of social convention. She does not save Helen Burns, for instance, whose tendency to self-sacrifice leads to her eventual death, or Eliza Reed who ends up, unsatisfactorily as far as Jane is concerned, in a convent. Most of the other women from her class – including Miss Temple, Miss Oliver and Georgiana Reed – marry according to the prevailing custom of the day by making slightly compromising matches, and we do not even know what happens to others – Miss Ingram, for instance, vanishes without trace.

## THE MARRIAGE MARKET

As well as being a governess, Jane (like Charlotte Brontë) was the daughter of a clergyman. Clergymen have always and still do hold a peculiarly ambivalent position in English society, being well educated, having high aspirations, and often the younger sons of 'good families', but *poor*. As a consequence the daughters of clergymen, while frequently mixing with the upper classes would not have been countenanced as potential spouses, either by the upper classes or often even by the middle classes, as they brought no dowry with them. This is why – on a more mundane level – one of the themes of the novel is therefore the 'marriage market'. In this respect the book ends happily because the 'good' win out and find

**CONTEXT**

Until the 1870 Education Act there were several types of school, private (run by individuals), National Schools (run by the Church of England), British and Foreign schools (run by nonconformist churches), endowed (i.e. charitable), and ragged run by the Ragged School Union for the poor from 1844.

**CONTEXT**

Charlotte Brontë
was the daughter
of a clergyman.
She received three
proposals during
her life, but finally
married her
father's curate,
Arthur Bell
Nicholls, in 1854.
She died during
pregnancy a few
months later, in
March 1855.

husbands Jane does, and so do Diana and Mary, Miss Temple and
Miss Oliver.

However, in order for this to happen, the would-be brides must
have money. This is why Mr Rochester was quite prepared to marry
a foreigner whom he hardly knew – he was offered a large sum of
money to do so – why it is so seemingly remarkable that Mr
Rochester first proposes to Jane and rejects Miss Ingram, and,
ironically, only legitimately proposes to Jane after their discussion
of her inheritance; why after Jane inherits, she is deemed by St John
to be a fitting spouse; and why Diana and Mary can marry once
Jane has handed over part of her fortune. Jane's fortune,
incidentally, would roughly equal a million pounds in today's
money.

## QUEST FOR LOVE

A further, obvious, theme is Jane's quest for love. Before the novel
has even begun Jane has lost the love of her natural parents, as well
as that of her uncle, through their respective deaths. Belatedly, she
finds a degree of maternal love in Bessie, but quickly loses it again as
she is taken off to school at Lowood. She has never experienced any
kind of affection from her cousins, but seems to find a sisterly love
in Helen Burns, who then dies. Again, she finds a motherly love in
Miss Temple, but she loses this when her mentor leaves. Jane
therefore decides to move on and once more seems to find a kind of
motherly love in Mrs Fairfax, and herself becomes a mother-figure
for little Adèle. Mr Rochester, in the meantime, seems to become a
dangerous father-figure who then betrays her. She therefore flees
Thornfield and finally discovers a lasting sisterly love with Diana
and Mary. She at first finds a brotherly love in St John, but soon
loses this when he proposes to her. Eventually, of course, Jane finds
a passionate and companionable love with Rochester, now reduced
to her level through his injuries, blindness and loss of property. One
message here seems to be that life and love are basically cruel and
that happiness can only truly be achieved at a price. However,
Brontë also seems to attack the convention of brotherly and sisterly
love as the basis for marriage here, in favour of the new ideal of
companionship.

## RELIGIOUS FAITH

The novel also, at its core, deals with religious faith – hence the uproar amongst Evangelicals when it was published. It addresses the meaning of religion and its relevance to the individual's behaviour. Jane sees the best and the worst of religious practice at Lowood, encounters a man who wants to reform morality for his own convenience at Thornfield and is finally subject to the juggernaut of religious self-sacrifice at Moor House. Every character who professes some kind of religious faith is placed and subject to some form of ironic commentary. It becomes clear that convention based on social propriety can all too easily be confused with customary behaviour based on religious doctrine. And the novel asks if morality can simply be remade as a social convention, or whether it is something more.

## NARRATIVE TECHNIQUES

### STRUCTURE

The novel is very tightly constructed and the form has been dictated by its major theme. There is a certain amount of coincidence at work, but only to the extent that coincidences also happen in real life. Brontë wanted to write about what is 'true', in other words what is deeply felt, genuine and sincere, as much as what is observed or 'real' and we can see this in the composition of the novel as much as in its content.

This novel's structure is deceptively organic and free-flowing, and lacks a moral framework which marks a radical departure from the novel dominant in Brontë's day. In effect it is given structural unity by Jane, who carries the theme while she searches for a way to build her own identity and resolve the tensions within her character. Because of this and her movements to and from Thornfield, the book falls roughly into five phases, which do not quite correspond with the three volumes of the original edition.

At the end of each phase Jane moves on to a new stage in her development at Gateshead she is still a child; when she leaves for

**CONTEXT**

The period 1833–45 saw widespread religious debate about 'Tractarianism', also known as High Church Anglicanism and the Oxford Movement. This was lead by John Henry Newman, who finally converted to the Catholic Church in 1845. As the daughter of a clergyman, Charlotte would have been well aware of this debate.

Lowood she moves into girlhood; she is an adolescent at Thornfield; reaches maturity at Marsh End; and becomes fulfilled with her marriage to Rochester at Ferndean. This structure is suggestive of growth and supports the theme by showing the reader how Jane develops. The structure of the novel is therefore effectively that of a *Bildungsroman*, or 'novel of development', in which the protagonist's growth is traced through childhood, into adulthood and maturity. This is apt given the novel's subtitle '*An Autobiography*'.

**QUESTION**

How does the narrative structure of *Jane Eyre* compare to other 'classic' novels?

There is also some repetition in the novel, however, especially in Jane's flight from Edward Rochester and her flight from St John Rivers, which provides it with an alternative or parallel framework. In the thematic structure of the novel, the Jane–Rivers relationship develops in direct contrast to the Jane–Rochester relationship. This enables us to see exactly what is at stake for Jane, who must resolve the tension between passion and self-control in order to live a happy and fulfilled life. On both occasions she struggles to maintain her identity and the two characters effectively symbolise different aspects of her-*self*. The parallels are made clear when she says 'I was almost as hard beset by him [St John] as I had been once before, in a different way, by another' (Vol. III, Ch. 9, p. 465).

## NARRATIVE AND POINT OF VIEW

The narrative focuses entirely on Jane, events only appear in the book because they have an impact on her growth into an independent, moral and strong-minded woman and we are only interested in other characters' experiences because Jane can learn from them. Every character and incident therefore has some bearing on her development and, in this way, the theme of the novel is brought alive; every detail is made to count. We are never surprised by a new development of Jane's character each phase, each element of character development is given a sound basis earlier on in the novel. Plot and character are **foreshadowed**.

Because the novel is a fictional autobiography and therefore consists of a first-person narrative we largely see events and characters from the narrator's point of view and this gives the story a high degree of authenticity. This also creates a very close bond between the narrator and the reader and draws the latter into a closer involvement with the story. These petitions to the reader always come at moments of heightened intensity or action, for example when Rochester asks Jane to forgive him after their first wedding-day, 'Reader, I forgave him' (Vol. III, Ch. 1, p. 336), when Jane runs away from Rochester afterwards, 'Gentle reader, may you never feel what I felt!' (Vol. III, Ch. 1, p. 361), and as we come to the close of the novel, 'Reader, I married him' (Vol. III, Ch. 12, p. 498).

As we have seen in respect of the structure of the novel, it falls roughly into five parts. This works because the novel is set in five different locales Gateshead, Lowood, Thornfield, Moor House and Ferndean Manor. Each time Jane moves from one locale to another the narrative breaks to set the scene and stress that this setting will form a new stage in Jane's life. It is as if we were moving from one act to another in a five-act drama – an analogy the narrator uses herself in Volume I, Chapter 11. There are also two scenes in which Jane travels back to a previous locale from Thornfield to Gateshead, to visit her aunt, and from Moor House to Thornfield, when she searches for Rochester.

Each setting is dominated by a different tone. At Gateshead, for instance, the tone is passionate, superstitious and wild. This reflects the fact that the narrative is focused on a child at this point and shows us the more irrational elements in Jane's character. The tone at Lowood is cold, hard and constrained and reflects the limitations placed on young women by religious thought and social convention. At Thornfield the setting is personal and symbolic, for instance the house itself is identified with Rochester, and the narrative veers between the pacy and the restrained. We feel Jane's pulse quickening as she begins to fall in love with her master, but we are also given a sense of the way in which she is torn between passion and self-control. At Moor House the tone again becomes more stifling and oppressive as Jane slips back into a more conventional way of behaving, and begins to feel the limitations and killing pressure of St John's urge to self-sacrifice. However, when we finally reach Ferndean we move at last from fear and anticipation to delight. The novel therefore oscillates between the irrational – Gateshead and Thornfield – and the rational – Lowood

 **QUESTION**

Consider the ways in which Thornfield's architecture represents Jane's psychological state and its master's condition.

and Moor House – reflecting the divisions within Jane herself, until resolution is achieved at Ferndean.

## LANGUAGE AND STYLE

**CONTEXT**

Her use of the word 'idol' draws our attention to the Bible's Ten Commandments. Different versions of the Christian Church number them slightly differently, and they are worded slightly differently in Exodus and Deuteronomy, but as an Anglican, Brontë would have been familiar with two commandments referring to false worship. In this case, Jane is referring to the Second Commandment 'Thou shalt not make unto thee any graven image' (from the Holy Bible, King James version, Exodus 20:3–18).

Brontë wrote very carefully, drafting out every passage before writing it up and she spent a considerable amount of time on small details such as the choice of names. 'Eyre', for instance, came from the Eyre family whose historic house had a room in it which had housed a madwoman, but Brontë used the name because it carried with it the sense of being as free as air, a faint reference to the sprite Ariel and the suggestion of an eagle's eyrie. Where the name 'Reed' suggests a certain pliability, 'Rivers' suggests the pull of strong currents and the influence of forces beyond the individual's control. 'Temple' suggests a place of worship, safety and goodness. 'Jane' hints at 'plain Jane'.

Brontë's language is deceptively simple. Because of her upbringing and early reading, it often has a faintly archaic, eighteenth-century feel to it and tends to be a blend of literary English and Yorkshire dialect. For example, 'e'en took the poor thing' in Volume I, Chapter 15 (p. 164). This has presented editors with considerable difficulty when correcting her text for publication. For instance, in Volume III, Chapter 9 Diana says to Jane 'Tell me what business St John and you have on hands' (Vol. III, Ch. 9, p. 461) This is often changed to 'on hand', but may actually be a local colloquialism.

The descriptive passages of the novel draw us into the action, and though their style is often quite journalistic – 'It was the fifteenth of January, about nine o'clock in the morning Bessie was gone down to breakfast; my cousins had not yet been summoned to their mama' (Vol. I, Ch. 4, p. 38) – they are highly suggestive. 'Terrible moment full of struggle, blackness, burning! Not a human being that ever lived could wish to be loved better than I was loved; and him who thus loved me I absolutely worshipped and I must renounce love and idol' (Vol. III, Ch. 1, p. 354).

The dialogue is especially important because it reflects the education, station and attitude of the characters; with respect to

Adèle it is also indicative of her nationality and training. The extensive use of French in the novel adds veracity to Adèle's exchanges with Jane and makes Jane's own accomplishments more tangible. The dialogue also allows us an insight into the minds of the characters, brings them alive and is generally much more convincing than anything written by Brontë's predecessors.

The conversations between Jane and Rochester, for example, feel entirely natural and give us a real sense of their love for each other. Jane and Rochester express themselves very directly, and everything from their banter to their most impassioned exchanges is suggestive of deeply felt and genuine affection. It is also interesting to see how Jane automatically corrects Hannah's English when she first talks to the servant as her superior in Volume III, Chapter 3:

'I am no beggar; any more than yourself or your young ladies.'

After a pause, she said, 'I dunnut understand that you've like no house, nor no brass, I guess?'

'The want of house or brass (by which I suppose you mean money) does not make a beggar in your sense of the word.'

(p. 381)

This suggests that Jane is acutely sensitive of her social position at this point, and hints at the snobbery of her childhood when she could not 'purchase liberty at the price of caste' (Vol. I, Ch. 3, p. 32).

Brontë's language is at its most powerful when she is describing a mind in torment. The heart of the novel therefore lies in Jane's descriptions of what is going on in her own mind. Her feelings, especially 'conscience' and 'passion' (Vol. III, Ch. 1, p. 335), are often given their own voice and they frequently act out a kind of drama or inner morality play within Jane, in which they fight over the right to determine her actions. Volume III, Chapter 1, in which Jane determines to leave Rochester, provides us with an excellent example of this. These moments of **personification** make us aware of Jane's deepest feelings and help us to understand why she acts as she does.

> **CONTEXT**
>
> The use of French and references to other languages are indicative of the level of education Charlotte and her readers possessed.

> **CONTEXT**
>
> Despite her subversive tendencies, Jane still reflects many of the dominant attitudes of her class and time. Charlotte could also be a snob; she looked down, for instance, on one of her father's curates – who proposed to her – because he came from Dublin and was therefore not, in her view, her social equal.

**CONTEXT**

The **Romantics**
rejected the
limitations of form
and precedent and
saw themselves as
individuals who
could express
themselves
according to their
imagination. They
explored
everything that
was felt to be
mysterious,
remote, unnerving,
and assumed the
mantle of prophets
and legislators; the
poet became a
special kind of
person, set apart
from other people
because of them.
They saw nature as
unmodified by
humanity,
inherently dazzling
and elevating; and
believed that
humanity should
learn from nature
personified as
'Nature'.

# IMAGERY AND SYMBOLISM

Imagery and symbolism help unite the novel and are as important to the narrative as the action and plot. The novel is full of uncanny, faintly gothic, references to local folklore, fairytales, ghosts and sprites. Jane is driven back to Rochester when she mysteriously hears his voice calling to her when St John Rivers presses her to marry him. But, as noted in **Language and style**, the core of the novel actually lies in Jane's descriptions of what goes on in her mind and it is in these descriptions that we find Brontë's most striking use of imagery.

Brontë gets her imagery from literature, especially from Shakespeare and the **Romantics**, the Bible, and, for the large supernatural element in the novel, from her own upbringing. Some images are quite commonplace, but nonetheless when repeated help form clear links between the various characters. Rochester often likens Jane to an eager little bird, for example, meaning she is physically small and mentally agile, but Jane also likens herself to the 'stray and stranger birds' (Vol. II, Ch. 7, p. 275) that Rochester throws his crumbs to. After Jane has run away from Rochester, her heart becomes 'impotent as a bird' which, 'with both wings broken … still quivered its shattered pinions in vain attempts to seek him' (Vol. III, Ch. 2, p. 364). And when the Rivers offer her a home, St John likens her to 'a half-frozen bird, which some wintry wind might have driven through their casement' (Vol. III, Ch. 3, p. 390). When she returns to Rochester she finds that he is like a 'fettered wild beast or bird,' and that, as they enter the final stage of their relationship in which he has to depend on her, he has become 'a royal eagle, chained to a perch' which is 'forced to entreat a sparrow to become its purveyor' (Vol. III, Ch. 11, p. 488).

Another imaginative link, which draws more directly on Brontë's knowledge of folklore, is formed between Jane and Bertha. When Jane sees herself in the mirror of the red-room she sees herself as a ghost, and she is referred to as a sprite and a witch by Rochester. These are quite playful references to the supernatural, but they take on a new import when she herself describes Bertha as a vampire.

This feeds into the **Gothic** tone of the Thornfield section of the text and shows us how Jane might herself fall victim to her passions to become another Bertha.

It is interesting to see how Thornfield Hall is often symbolically identified with its master, in appearance, and when it is destroyed. One of the most powerful images in the novel is that of the shattered chestnut tree that stands in its grounds. This tree initially stands as an omen. As a symbol of life it is quite fitting that Rochester proposes to Jane under its boughs. However, split in two by a violent storm that very night it suddenly forewarns us of the disaster to come, of the failed wedding-day and Mr Rochester's injury, and as such fills Jane's thoughts with foreboding before their wedding. It finally reappears at the end of the novel when Rochester proposes for the second time 'I am no better than the old lightning-struck chestnut-tree in Thornfield orchard' (Vol. III, Ch. 11, p. 493). In other words the tree, initially a simple object in the novel, is transformed by events into a complex image and powerful symbol of Jane and Rochester's relationship.

A key feature of the novel is the symbolic use of literature. We learn a lot about the characters and their situation from what they read. The novel opens on a depressing November afternoon which reflects the depression of Jane Eyre herself who is trying to escape by reading Bewick's *British Birds*. This book is full of images of shipwrecks, storms, Arctic wastes, high mountain reaches, death and disaster and it seems to reflect Jane's own feelings about life at Gateshead. She also reads *Gulliver's Travels* as a kind of escape and the *Arabian Nights* where she learns about magic. Helen Burns, however, prefers *Rasselas*, a very dry tome about the placid endurance of life and reality. Whereas Jane prefers to read texts that feed into her passions, Helen hopes to learn about the real world and the necessity of self-control.

**QUESTION**

In what ways does Brontë draw on classic literary forms and genres, such as the fairytale, **Romantic** literature or the **Gothic**?

**CONTEXT**

The image of a storm is a reminder that shipwrecks were frequently used to signal disaster in Victorian novels.

# PART FOUR

# CRITICAL HISTORY

## RECEPTION AND EARLY CRITICAL REVIEWS

*Jane Eyre* was well received and a bestseller when it was first published. But there was also widespread censure of the novel on social and moral grounds due to its critical representation of religious sentiment, its easy acceptance of a love which transcends class, and, finally, its author's vivid portrayal of emotion. Elizabeth Rigby, for instance, writing for a conservative periodical, the *Quarterly Review* in 1848, felt that 'the tone of mind and thought which has overthrown authority and violated every code human and divine … is the same which has also written *Jane Eyre*'.

Thus, in the 1840s, *Jane Eyre* was a revolutionary text. Victorian critics did not like Jane Eyre's strong-minded independence and many thought that the novel was coarse. The novel was blamed for the corruption of contemporary tastes and morality, in both life and art. Most contemporary critics felt that there was something dangerous in the novel's underlying message, while Jane Eyre herself was seen as godless and unrestrained. Others thought that Brontë's personality was reflected in the novel and that that personality was irredeemably coarse, vulgar and alien.

Such a view was only changed after Mrs Gaskell's biography of Charlotte Brontë was published, and Charlotte Brontë herself worked hard at rescuing the reputation of the book.

**CHECK THE BOOK**

For a discussion of the ways in which Charlotte's reputation, that of *Jane Eyre* and that of Jane have been intertwined, see Lucasta Miller *The Brontë Myth* (2002).

## EARLY TWENTIETH-CENTURY VIEWS

Up until the 1970s twentieth-century critics like Lord David Cecil in *Early Victorian Novelists* (Constable, 1934) were quite scathing in their assessment of *Jane Eyre* because of the way in which the novel operates, in part, as a fairytale or as a simple narrative of wish fulfilment. This, in their view, put the novel beyond the bounds of a serious adult readership while, at the same time, they accused it of being a baggy, rather artless blend of undisciplined daydreams. Brontë was supposed to have written incoherently, without form, restraint, observation or analysis. The narrative was said to be held up by unnecessary passages of over-poetic prose. The plot was accused of moving forward thanks to a combination of good luck and coincidence, while the novel itself was assumed to lack composition. However, others, like Q.D. Leavis in her introduction to the Penguin edition of *Jane Eyre* in 1966, stood up for the novel and argued that it was in fact very tightly composed, and that its structure was coherent and thoroughly controlled in the interest of the theme. In it, Jane Eyre's world, her thoughts and feelings are, it was argued, not simply observed, but, more importantly, imagined on the deepest level.

**CHECK THE NET**

The Victorian Web has extensive commentaries and further background information on *Jane Eyre*, Charlotte Brontë and her period **http://www. victorianweb.org/** — go to Authors and click on Charlotte Brontë.

## MARXIST CRITICISM

During the 1970s new readings of the novel began to emerge, most notably those of Marxists and feminists. Marxist critics, like Raymond Williams in *The English Novel from Dickens to Lawrence* (1970) and Terry Eagleton in *Myths of Power a Marxist study of the Brontës* (1975), reassessed the context in which Brontë's books were written and read. They exhibited an interest in the ambiguity of Jane's social position as governess and her social mobility, which belied the paradoxes and ideological fissures of Brontë's own time. Williams stressed that the period in which the Brontë sisters were writing was one of unprecedented social change. The tensions of this period, he argued, are reflected both in the representation of desire and in the fear of isolation that we see in *Jane Eyre*. The novel's passion is then communicated through a kind of private conversation between narrator and reader and this, in his view, is what makes it new. Eagleton, in turn, argued that the central problem or key theme in *Jane Eyre* is submission and the point at which this ceases to be a good thing. Charlotte Brontë, in Eagleton's view, sought a balance between the social and moral conventions of her day and self-fulfilment. Due to this, in *Jane Eyre*, Jane negotiates her way between these opposing urges and manages to climb the social ladder, quite properly – thanks to an inheritance and good behaviour – *and* on her own terms.

**CHECK THE BOOK**

For a feminist analysis of Jean Rhys' *Wide Sargasso Sea* and other work see M. Humm *Border Traffic strategies of contemporary women writers* (1991).

**CHECK THE FILM**

Jean Rhys' *Wide Sargasso Sea* was made into an atmospheric and highly charged film by John Duigan in 1993.

# FEMINIST CRITICISM

Feminist critics, in their turn, read *Jane Eyre* as a radical text in which a woman writer wrote successfully about the treatment of women in her society. In this way feminists, like Sandra Gilbert and Susan Gubar in *The Madwoman in the Attic: The Woman Writer and the Nineteenth-Century Literary Imagination* (1979), picked up on the issues that so distressed the book's original, Victorian critics. Most commentators in fact now tend to stress the underlying political purpose of the novel in which Jane acts as an advocate for women. This works because, though the plot is like that of a fairytale, it has been transposed to the real material world of wages and work in which Cinderella's story has quite different and has much more radical implications to those it has when it is safely tucked away in never-never land. Gilbert and Gubar therefore say that Mrs Rigby's assessment of *Jane Eyre*, quoted above, is quite correct, whether or not the author wanted to admit it at the time.

Not all criticism comes in the form of non-fiction prose, of course, and *Jane Eyre* has also been replied to in the form of prequel. Jean Rhys' *The Wide Sargasso Sea* (1966) tells the story of Rochester's life in the Caribbean from the first Mrs Rochester's point of view, rather than Jane's, and provides the reader with a very different understanding of the original narrative.

## CONTEMPORARY APPROACHES

Psychoanalytical readings and those which focus on myth have suggested many new and interesting readings of the novel, including the idea that Rochester's first wife is Jane's double. Bertha Mason is a madwoman who is kept under lock and key in the attic, is unable to speak, physically and mentally resembles a savage wild animal and is treated as a thing rather than as a human being. She therefore seems to be the opposite of Jane who is a calm English governess, rational, self-controlled, articulate and small. However, as Elizabeth Imlay has noted in *Charlotte Brontë and the Mysteries of Love Myth and Allegory in Jane Eyre* (1989), both women are represented at different times in very similar ways.

Jane describes Bertha as a ghost or a vampire after the wedding veil is torn. This is a very frightening image, but Mr Rochester similarly thinks of Jane as an imp, spirit and witch. Bertha is mad, and Jane is said to behave like a mad cat; Bertha scratches and bites, and Jane scratches her cousin John Reed; Bertha is tied to a chair and locked in a room, Jane is told to sit in a chair and is locked in the red-room. In other words, when Jane follows her passions and loses her self-control, she behaves and is punished like Bertha. When she is frustrated by her life at Thornfield Jane goes up onto the third floor to daydream, at which point she is physically and mentally close to Bertha. In this way we become aware of the fact that Jane could easily become another madwoman if she followed her basest instincts. Bertha's death, at which point Rochester is also maimed and tamed, therefore symbolises the sacrifice of the most passionate part of Jane's self.

However, Gayatri Spivak in *Critical Inquiry* 12 (1) 1985, criticised this kind of approach and argued that Jane Eyre's rise as an independent woman was dependent upon the fall and dehumanisation of a colonial subject. Also, that the novel therefore reflected the patterns of imperialism. Edward Said in *Orientalism* (1978) had by this point highlighted the importance of colonialism and images of imperialism and empire in *Jane Eyre*. Jane is clearly a white middle-class Protestant who believes in healthy good deeds and hard work. When she runs away from Thornfield she therefore says that she will try to turn her hand to anything that is honest. However, she still draws the line at travelling to India where, she fears, she would collapse and die, as St John eventually does. This rational approach to life allows her to have the self-control that Bertha Mason lacks.

Bertha Mason's story is itself a colonial narrative. Rochester marries her purely for her property. In fact, he went to the Caribbean just to seek his fortune and, like other English adventurers, found unbridled passion and madness as well as a solution to his financial difficulties. Interestingly, until Rochester meets Jane all his sexual partners have been foreign, and this is typical of the period. Foreign women were supposed to be more highly sexed than English women, but, more importantly, the very fact that they were foreign

**CHECK THE FILM**

The best twentieth-century film and stage versions of the novel, those like Franco Zeffireli's 1996 version that capture its underlying emotion and sexual tension, were influenced by contemporary, post-Freudian, interpretations of the novel. But it is important to go back to the book as adaptations will say more about the time at which they are made than they will about the original text.

**CHECK THE BOOK**

For a general study of post-colonial writing, to which genre and period Jean Rhys' work belongs, see B. Ashcroft, G. Griffiths and H. Tiffin *The Empire Writes Back Theory and Practice in Post-Colonial Literatures* (1998).

also made them particularly attractive to English men. Foreign shores and people were seen as dangerous, essentially unhealthy, wild, yet alluring in the British novels of the time, and Charlotte Brontë has made full use of this widespread colonial imagery. Bertha is treated and seen as a thing rather than a human being because she is a Creole, not just because she is a madwoman. And, as suggested by Rochester's desperate need to leave the West Indies, it is suggested that only Britain can provide a safe haven for the English.

More recently still, critics like Peter Hulme in *Colonial Discourse/Postcolonial Theory* (1994), have stressed that though it remains important to take a critical view of *Jane Eyre* in light of Jean Rhys' novel, Jean Rhys herself can be categorised as a member of the 'white colonial elite', while her novel is 'sympathetic to the planter class ruined by emancipation'.

# PART FIVE

## BACKGROUND

## CHARLOTTE BRONTË AND HER WORKS

Charlotte Brontë (1816–55) was the third of five daughters born to Patrick Brontë and Maria Branwell. Born in Northern Ireland Patrick Brontë had taken a scholarship in England to become a Church of England clergyman and, after working as a curate, finally became Rector of Haworth on the Yorkshire Moors in 1820. Her mother and Aunt Elizabeth came from a prominent Cornish, Methodist family. Charlotte's younger sisters, Anne and Emily Brontë, also became authors. Their mother died in 1821 and after this they and their brother Branwell were looked after by their mother's sister Elizabeth Branwell.

Charlotte was initially educated at home, then sent to a boarding school for clergymen's daughters at Cowan Bridge with her two elder sisters Maria and Elizabeth, and Emily. Maria and Elizabeth died of tuberculosis there in 1825. Because their illness had been made worse by lack of food and the unhealthy conditions at the school Charlotte and Emily were removed. Charlotte then stayed at home for several years. During this time she read widely with her family and invented an imaginary world with Branwell called Angria. Charlotte, Emily, Anne and Branwell wrote a large amount of poetry, drama and prose over this period, 1829–31.

In 1831 Charlotte went to Miss Wooler's school at Roe Head, where she became an assistant teacher in 1835. She disliked the work and, from 1839 to 1841, attempted to make a living as a governess. She and her sisters hoped in the long run to open their own school and, with her aunt's help, she and Emily travelled to Brussels in 1842 in order to study languages. They returned at the end of the year due to her aunt's illness. During this time they had had no enquiries about their school, so Charlotte went back to Brussels on her own in 1843 to work as an English teacher. During this time her letters reveal that she became close to her tutor Monsieur Heger.

 **CHECK THE NET**

For information about the Brontë family and their home, which includes information about the Brontë Society, see the Brontë Parsonage Museum site **http://www.bronte.info/**

**CONTEXT**

The 1830s and 1840s were a time of considerable social unrest, while 1840s became known widely as 'the Hungry Forties'.

# CHARLOTTE BRONTË AND HER WORKS Background

Charlotte returned home in 1844 in order to care for her father who, by this point, was nearly blind. Shortly after this she discovered her sister Emily's poetry in 1845. Charlotte had already begun to write her own verse, so she organised the publication in 1846 of *Poems by Currer, Ellis and Acton Bell* – the assumed names of Charlotte, Emily and Anne. The verse did not sell well and Charlotte's first novel *The Professor* which she began in 1846 was not published until much later, but *Jane Eyre* (1847) was an immediate success.

Branwell and Emily died in 1848, followed by Anne in 1849, but Charlotte continued to write. Charlotte also published *Shirley*, a condition of England novel set in Yorkshire during the period of the Luddite riots at the end of the Napoleonic era. This was followed by *Villette* (1853) and *The Professor* (1857) both of which draw on her life in Brussels – *The Professor* having been written before *Jane Eyre*. She visited London in 1849, 1850, 1851 and 1853 and made her mark on the literary circles of her day. It was during this period of her life that Charlotte met Thackeray, to whom she had dedicated *Jane Eyre*, G.H. Lewes, and Harriet Martineau, and became friends with her future biographer Elizabeth Gaskell. Though some critics said Charlotte was too 'strong-minded' and coarse, she was generally recognised as a powerful and talented writer by her contemporaries.

## HISTORICAL BACKGROUND

Jane Eyre is an advocate for her sex at a time when women's talents, skills and independence were far from being valued. Charlotte Brontë was well aware of women's subservient position in Victorian society and of the difficulties that were faced by a woman who wanted or had to make her way in the world. At this point it was not respectable for a middle-class woman to earn her own living she was expected to make a career out of marriage or at least to confine her public interests to doing unpaid charitable work. If a young middle-class woman had to support herself and wanted to maintain her class position and reputation, she really only had one option to work as a governess. The governess was therefore in an anomalous social position because she was neither a servant, due to her class, nor a proper young lady.

Brontë was especially sensitive to the difficulties faced by these young women because she herself had worked as a teacher and as a governess, and hoped to make a career out of writing. This lends a special poignancy to Jane's story as in many respects it was based on Charlotte Brontë's own experience. Brontë also read widely on the subject of woman's position thanks to the large number of articles and books that were being published on this issue in the 1840s. It would not be useful to overemphasise the significance of the author's biography here, Brontë herself said that though Jane Eyre looked like her, they had nothing else in common, but the theme of the novel was deeply felt by Brontë and this should be borne in mind.

Other than this, Brontë draws relatively sketchily on the history of the time at which the novel is set – around the turn of the eighteenth to nineteenth centuries. This was a period of considerable social unrest; there was widespread concern that the British labourer would go the way of the French in the Revolution of 1789. When Jane comments adversely on her pupil's French disposition, she is therefore expressing the sceptical views of her time, this being the period of the French wars (ending in 1815). In similar vein, there are also various allusions to the French Revolution in, for example, Volume III, Chapter 7 'Famous equality and fraternization' (p. 432) speaks obliquely of the slogan 'Liberty, Equality, Fraternity'. Beyond this, there are very few historical references.

The novel does draw extensively on the imperial context. For instance, the slave trade had only been abolished in 1807 in British territories, after a long-fought campaign by a number of organisations including the Quakers, while emancipation was only achieved in 1833. During the period 1781-1807 Britain had carried in excess of a million slaves from Africa to the Americas. As a 'Creole', Bertha Mason would probably have counted slaves traded by France – which initially abolished slavery during the Revolution – among her ancestors. Beyond this we have references to trade with the Caribbean and missionary activity in India, including Jane's comment that 'I was not heroic enough to purchase liberty at the

**CHECK THE BOOK**

For more detail on the cultural background to the novel see R. Gilmour *The Victorian Period the Intellectual and Cultural Context of English literature 1830–1890* (1993).

**CONTEXT**

Jane refers to 'caste' (Vol. I. Ch. 3, p. 32) in reflecting on her future. Caste was an Indian concept that drew on a hierarchy that was religious, as well as social and economic, and one that was designated by birth rather than experience.

price of caste' (Vol. I, Ch. 3, p. 32) – all part of the economic, political and social context in which Brontë was writing.

## LITERARY BACKGROUND

**CHECK THE BOOK**

For more on the general prose context of the period see H. Fraser with D. Brown *English Prose of the Nineteenth Century* (1996).

Charlotte Brontë read widely as a child and as a young woman while she lived at home in her father's rectory at Haworth. She, her brother and sisters were encouraged to dip into Aesop, the Bible, Homer, Virgil, Shakespeare, Milton, Thomson, Goldsmith, Pope, Byron, Scott, Southey, Wordsworth, *The Arabian Nights' Entertainments*, Campbell, plus critical and political articles published in periodicals such as *Blackwood's Magazine*, *Fraser's Magazine*, and *The Edinburgh Review*. They also read from illustrated annuals such as *The Gem*, *The Amulet*, and *Friendship's Offering*.

Charlotte Brontë may have lost the strong religious sensibility of her earlier years by the time that she wrote *Jane Eyre*, but her early literary training continued to be influential in all her novels. The sagas, poetry and dramas that the Brontë children wrote provide ample evidence of the influence of this diverse reading and are full of **melodrama**, passion, the weird and wonderful, and keenly felt moral themes. This helps explain why *Jane Eyre* seems to be a mixture of the **Gothic, realist** and **Romantic**.

**CHECK THE NET**

A reliable e-text of Mrs Gaskell's *The Life of Charlotte Brontë* (1857) can be found at the Project Gutenberg site **http:// promo.net/pg/** — search for Gaskell under Authors and 'Life of Charlotte Brontë' under Title Word(s).

Charlotte continued to read widely throughout her lifetime but there do appear to be some interesting gaps in her literary history. For instance, at the time that *Jane Eyre* was being written, Jane Austen was already a well-established author, but it does not appear that Charlotte had read her. The critic G.H. Lewes in fact advised Charlotte to read some of Austen's work in order to improve her own writing. When Charlotte finished *Pride and Prejudice*, however, she wrote to Lewes explaining that Austen was altogether useless to her and was not even, really, a novelist, as she was 'without poetry'. Austen, Brontë argued, was 'only shrewd and observant', she was 'sensible, real (more *real* than *true*) but she cannot be great'. It is difficult to know exactly who Charlotte

Brontë read in later life, but we know from the dedication which appears in the second edition that she read Thackeray who, like Trollope, George Eliot and Dickens, shared her dislike of Evangelicalism, while Mrs Gaskell was of course her friend and later her biographer.

 **CHECK THE NET**
Voice of the Shuttle is a good place to find further resources **http://vos.ucsb. edu/** — search by title and or author.

| World events | Charlotte's life | Literary events |
|---|---|---|
| **1811** First Luddite riot, Nottingham | | |
| | **1812** Patrick Brontë, an Irish Protestant clergyman marries Maria Branwell, a Cornish Methodist from Penzance | |
| | **1813** Birth of Maria | **1813** Jane Austen, *Pride and Prejudice* |
| **1813-17** Luddites executed, York. Movement broken | **1813-18** Patrick publishes a collection of poems and two novels | |
| **1815** Napoleon escapes from Elba, becomes Emperor and is defeated at Waterloo | **1815** Birth of Elizabeth | **1815** Byron, *Completed Works* |
| | **1816** Birth of Charlotte | **1816** Jane Austen, *Emma* |
| | **1817** Birth of Branwell | **1817** Death of Jane Austen |
| | **1818** Birth of Emily | **1818** Mary Shelley, *Frankenstein* |
| | **1819** The Brontë family move to Haworth in Yorkshire | |
| **1820** Death of George III (end of Regency), and accession of George IV, who attempts to dissolve his marriage to Caroline. Death of Napoleon | **1820** Birth of Anne | |
| | **1821** Mrs Maria Brontë dies of cancer, and her sister, Elizabeth Branwell, comes to care for the children | **1821** Death of poet, John Keats |
| | | **1824** Death of poet, Lord Byron |

| World events | Charlotte's life | Literary events |
|---|---|---|
| **1825** First railway opened between Stockton and Darlington | **1825** Both Maria and Elizabeth die of tuberculosis at Cowan Bridge School | |
| **1829** Catholic emancipation in Britain | | |
| **1830** Death of George IV and accession of William IV | | |
| **1830s** Abolitionists of Slave Trade active in America; articles in *Monthly Repository* by W.J. Fox and W.B. Adams influenced by Harriet Taylor | | |
| **1831** Cholera epidemic | **1831** Charlotte boards at Roe Head school, Mirfield | |
| **1832** First Reform Act | | **1832** Death of Walter Scott and Goethe; Harriet Martineau, *Illustrations of Political Economy*; Anna Jameson, *Characteristics of Women* |
| **1833** Slavery abolished | | |
| **1834** Establishment of Union Workhouses; Tolpuddle Martyrs | | |
| | **1835-8** Charlotte returns to Roe Head as a teacher, with Emily as a pupil, but after 3 months of homesickness Emily returns to Haworth | |
| | | **1836** Charles Dickens, *The Pickwick Papers* |
| **1837** Death of William IV; accession of Queen Victoria | | |

| World events | Charlotte's life | Literary events |
| --- | --- | --- |
| **1838** 'People's Charter' published | | |
| **1839** Chartist petition rejected by Parliament – riots, Birmingham | **1839** Charlotte, now a governess, visits Norton Conyers, near Rippon, model for Thornfield Hall, Charlotte turns down two proposals of marriage from her friend Ellen Nussey's clergyman brother, and from an Irish clergyman | |
| **1840** Penny Post established | | **1840** Death of novelist, Fanny Burney |
| | **1841** Charlotte becomes governess to a family near Bradford | |
| **1842** Second Chartist petition presented and rejected | **1842** Charlotte and Emily study French in Brussels at Mme Heger's school | |
| | **1843** Charlotte returns to Brussels to teach and falls in love with Monsieur Heger | **1843** Margaret Fuller (American journalist), 'The Great Lawsuit – Man versus Men. Woman versus Women', *The Dial* |
| | **1844** Charlotte returns home when her father becomes almost totally blind | |
| **1845** Newman converts to the Catholic faith | | **1845** Margaret Fuller, *Women in the Nineteenth Century* |
| **1845** Famine in Ireland due to potato blight | | |
| **1846** Repeal of Corn Laws | **1846** *Poems by Currer, Ellis and Acton Bell* are published by the three sisters | **1846** Margaret Fuller visits Britain |

| World events | Charlotte's life | Literary events |
|---|---|---|
| | **1847** Charlotte's *Jane Eyre* is published under the pseudonym of Currer Bell; Anne's *Agnes Grey* is published under the pseudonym of Acton Bell; Emily's *Wuthering Heights* is published under the pseudonym of Ellis Bell | **1847** William Thackeray, *Vanity Fair* (serialisation) |
| **1848** Final Chartist petition rejected. Revolutions in Paris, Berlin, Vienna, Venice, Rome, Milan, Naples, Prague and Budapest; Marx and Engel, *Communist Manifesto* | **1848** Anne's *The Tenant of Wildfell Hall* is published; Branwell dies of alcoholism; Emily dies of tuberculosis | **1848** Elizabeth Gaskell, *Mary Burton* |
| **1849** Cholera epidemic | **1849** Anne dies of tuberculosis, leaving Charlotte as the only surviving sibling. Charlotte publishes *Shirley* | **1849-54** *Eliza Cook's Journal* |
| **1851** The Great Exhibition at the Crystal Palace | **1849-51** Charlotte visits London and meets writers of her day; Mrs Gaskell, Harriet Martineau, William Thackeray | **1851** Harriet Taylor 'Enfranchisement of Women', in *Westminster Review* |
| | | **1852** Harriet Beecher Stowe, *Uncle Tom's Cabin* |
| | **1853** Charlotte publishes *Villette*, based on her experiences in Brussels | |
| **1854** Cholera epidemic | **1854** Charlotte marries her father's curate, Arthur Nicholls | |
| | **1855** Charlotte is pregnant, but dies from a combination of ill health and pneumonia, before reaching full term | |

Some general books on the Brontë sisters provide further useful insights

D. Ashcroft, G. Griffiths and H. Tiffin, *The Empire Writes Back Theory and Practice in Post-Colonial Literatures* (Routledge, 1998).
Post-colonial reading

P. Boumelha, *Charlotte Brontë*, Harvester, 1990
An excellent biography, as is Elizabeth Gaskell, *Life of Charlotte Brontë*, 1857, Penguin Classics, 1998

A. Carter, *The Bloody Chamber* (Gollancz, 1979).
Includes a rewriting of Bluebeard

A. Carter (ed.), *The Virago Book of Fairy Tales* (Virago, 1990).
Classic versions of fairy stories

A. Carter (ed.), *The Second Book of Virago Fairy Tales* (Virago, 1992).
Classic versions of fairy stories

L. Davidoff and C. Hall, *Family Fortunes: Men and Women of the English Middle Class 1780-1850* (2nd edn Routledge, 2002).
An excellent history of the period

T. Eagleton, *Myths of Power a Marxist Study of the Brontës* (Macmillan, 1975).
Marxist reading

Inga-Stina Ewbank, *Their Proper Sphere, A Study of the Brontë Sisters as Early-Victorian Female Novelists*, Edward Arnold, 1996
Places Charlotte and her sisters in their historical context

E. Figes, *Sex and Subterfuge: Women Writers to 1850* (Pandora, 1982).
Complex feminist readings of texts

H. Fraser with D. Brown, *English Prose of the Nineteenth Century* (Longman, 1996).
Good contextual survey

Mrs Gaskell, *The Life of Charlotte Brontë* (1857)
The first major biography. Very influential

S. M. Gilbert and S. Gubar, *The Madwoman in the Attic: The Woman Writer and the Nineteenth-Century Imagination* (Yale University Press, 1984).
Discusses relationship of author to subject

R. Gilmour, *The Victorian Period the Intellectual and Cultural Context of English Literature 1830-1890* (Longman, 1993).
Good contextual survey

P. Hulme, *Colonial Discourse/Postcolonial Theory* (Manchester University Press, 1994).
Post-colonial reading

M. Humm, *Border Traffic Strategies of Contemporary Women Writers* (Manchester University Press, 1991).
Complex feminist reading of *Wide Sargasso Sea*

E. Imlay, *Charlotte Brontë and the Mysteries of Love Myth and Allegory in Jane Eyre* (Harvester Wheatsheaf, 1989).
An imagery used by C. Brontë

Robert Bernard Martin, *The Accents of Persuasion; Charlotte Brontë's Novels*, Faber and Faber, 1966
A good traditional account

L. Miller, *The Brontë Myth* (Vintage, 2002).
How we've come to see the Brontës as we do

M. Poovey, *Uneven Developments the Ideological Work of Gender in Mid-Victorian England* (Virago, 1989).
Discusses history of governesses

Jean Rhys, *The Wide Sargasso Sea* (André Deutsch, 1966).
Rewriting of Bertha Mason's story

E. Said, *Orientalism* (Pantheon, 1978).
Post-colonial reading

Elaine Showalter, *A Literature of Their Own*, Princeton University Press, 1977
A useful introduction to women's writing in the nineteenth century

S. Shuttleworth, *Charlotte Brontë and Victorian Psychology* (Cambridge University Press, 1996).
Includes discussion of phrenology

G. C. Spivak, *Critical Inquiry* 12 (1) (1985).
Post-colonial reading

Tony Tanner, 'Passion, Narrative and Identity in *Wuthering Heights* and *Jane Eyre*', in *Contemporary Approaches to Narrative*, ed. Anthony Mortimer, Tübingen, 1984
A valuable survey of some of the key issues

N. D. Thompson, *Reviewing Sex Gender and the Reception of Victorian Novels* (Macmillan, 1996).
Includes discussion of the reception of *Jane Eyre*

M. Thormahlen, *The Brontës and Religion* (Cambridge University Press, 1999).

M. Waters, *The Garden in Victorian Literature* (Scolar Press, 1988).
Garden imagery

R. Williams, *The English Novel from Dickens to Lawrence* (Chatto & Windus, 1970).

R. Williams, *Keywords: A Vocabulary of Culture and Society* (Flamingo, 1983).
Useful history of language

*Bildüngsroman* is a 'coming of age' story, in other words a novel describing the progress of a character from childhood to maturity that focuses on the relationship between character, experience, education and identity. The *Bildungsroman* can be seen as a kind of underground confessional writing, which emerged at the turn of the eighteenth to nineteenth centuries. Other examples include C. Dickens' *David Copperfield* and *Great Expectations*

**denouement** means the final unfolding of the plot

**expository** comes from 'exposition', i.e. an explanation or to do with the delivery of information. Authors often use exposition to set the scene, but will tend to try and disguise it in order to maintain the reader's belief in the world that is being created. Information is therefore often smuggled in through conversation and other means

**foreshadowing** to be a sign of something to come; to suggest beforehand

**Gothic** Gothic novels are fictions that deal with cruel passions and supernatural terrors in some medieval setting, such as a haunted house or monastery. In their depiction of wild feelings they are both precursors and part of the literary movement called romanticism. Works with a similarly obsessive, gloomy, violent and spine-chilling atmosphere, but not necessarily with a medieval setting, are also called Gothic. Indeed, any work concentrating on the bizarre, the macabre or aberrant psychological states may be called Gothic

**irony** is a form of sarcasm. Saying one thing and meaning another. A norm is established and then subverted

**melodramatic** the word melodramatic itself comes from melodrama, which aimed to excite through incident and strong but simple feelings, with clearly 'good' or 'bad' characters and always ending happily

**Neoclassicism** the generalised beliefs of Neoclassical writers are based on the premise that the word is God's carefully ordered creation, with 'man' as a rational being capable of living harmoniously in society. Man's rational intelligence, common senses, was honoured and valued above al other faculties. Reason demonstrated that the great trusts about the world were well known, and fixed: the writer's duty was to express these truths in appropriate language. Unlike Romantics, Neoclassical writers did not value creativity or originality highly

**pathos** means suffering feeling; that quality in a work of art that arouses pity and sadness

**personification** is a figurative language in which ideas, feelings or things are treated as if they were human beings

**Realism** a realist author represents the world as it is rather than as it should be, using description rather than invention; observes and documents everyday life in straightforward prose; draws on characters from all levels of society, but often from the lowest classes; and represents their speech and manners accurately. Realism became the dominant form of literature in the nineteenth century

**Romantic** novels of the Romantic period are concerned with valuing feelings and emotion rather than the human capacity to reason. They are also interested in trying to explain a person's living relationship with the world around them including nature, landscape and their imagination.

Karen Sayer lectures in the Department of History at Trinity and All Saints College, University of Leeds. She took her first degree at Portsmouth Polytechnic and received her D.Phil. from the University of Sussex in 1991. Her first monograph *Women of the Fields* was published by Manchester University Press in 1995; her second *Country Cottages a Cultural History* was published by Manchester University Press in 2000.

## General editor

Martin Gray, former Head of the Department of English Studies at the University of Stirling, and of Literary Studies at the University of Luton.

Maya Angelou
*I Know Why the Caged Bird Sings*

Jane Austen
*Pride and Prejudice*

Alan Ayckbourn
*Absent Friends*

Elizabeth Barrett Browning
*Selected Poems*

Robert Bolt
*A Man for All Seasons*

Harold Brighouse
*Hobson's Choice*

Charlotte Brontë
*Jane Eyre*

Emily Brontë
*Wuthering Heights*

Shelagh Delaney
*A Taste of Honey*

Charles Dickens
*David Copperfield*
*Great Expectations*
*Hard Times*
*Oliver Twist*

Roddy Doyle
*Paddy Clarke Ha Ha Ha*

George Eliot
*Silas Marner*
*The Mill on the Floss*

Anne Frank
*The Diary of a Young Girl*

William Golding
*Lord of the Flies*

Oliver Goldsmith
*She Stoops to Conquer*

Willis Hall
*The Long and the Short and the Tall*

Thomas Hardy
*Far from the Madding Crowd*
*The Mayor of Casterbridge*
*Tess of the d'Urbervilles*
*The Withered Arm and other Wessex Tales*

L.P. Hartley
*The Go-Between*

Seamus Heaney
*Selected Poems*

Susan Hill
*I'm the King of the Castle*

Barry Hines
*A Kestrel for a Knave*

Louise Lawrence
*Children of the Dust*

Harper Lee
*To Kill a Mockingbird*

Laurie Lee
*Cider with Rosie*

Arthur Miller
*The Crucible*
*A View from the Bridge*

Robert O'Brien
*Z for Zachariah*

Frank O'Connor
*My Oedipus Complex and Other Stories*

George Orwell
*Animal Farm*

J.B. Priestley
*An Inspector Calls*
*When We Are Married*

Willy Russell
*Educating Rita*
*Our Day Out*

J.D. Salinger
*The Catcher in the Rye*

William Shakespeare
*Henry IV Part I*
*Henry V*
*Julius Caesar*
*Macbeth*
*The Merchant of Venice*
*A Midsummer Night's Dream*
*Much Ado About Nothing*

*Romeo and Juliet*
*The Tempest*
*Twelfth Night*

George Bernard Shaw
*Pygmalion*

Mary Shelley
*Frankenstein*

R.C. Sherriff
*Journey's End*

Rukshana Smith
*Salt on the snow*

John Steinbeck
*Of Mice and Men*

Robert Louis Stevenson
*Dr Jekyll and Mr Hyde*

Jonathan Swift
*Gulliver's Travels*

Robert Swindells
*Daz 4 Zoe*

Mildred D. Taylor
*Roll of Thunder, Hear My Cry*

Mark Twain
*Huckleberry Finn*

James Watson
*Talking in Whispers*

Edith Wharton
*Ethan Frome*

William Wordsworth
*Selected Poems*

*A Choice of Poets*

*Mystery Stories of the Nineteenth Century including The Signalman*

*Nineteenth Century Short Stories*

*Poetry of the First World War*

*Six Women Poets*

For the AQA Anthology:
*Duffy and Armitage & Pre-1914 Poetry*

*Heaney and Clarke & Pre-1914 Poetry*

*Poems from Different Cultures*

Margaret Atwood
*Cat's Eye*
*The Handmaid's Tale*

Jane Austen
*Emma*
*Mansfield Park*
*Persuasion*
*Pride and Prejudice*
*Sense and Sensibility*

Alan Bennett
*Talking Heads*

William Blake
*Songs of Innocence and of Experience*

Charlotte Brontë
*Jane Eyre*
*Villette*

Emily Brontë
*Wuthering Heights*

Angela Carter
*Nights at the Circus*

Geoffrey Chaucer
*The Franklin's Prologue and Tale*
*The Merchant's Prologue and Tale*
*The Miller's Prologue and Tale*
*The Prologue to the Canterbury Tales*
*The Wife of Bath's Prologue and Tale*

Samuel Coleridge
*Selected Poems*

Joseph Conrad
*Heart of Darkness*

Daniel Defoe
*Moll Flanders*

Charles Dickens
*Bleak House*
*Great Expectations*
*Hard Times*

Emily Dickinson
*Selected Poems*

John Donne
*Selected Poems*

Carol Ann Duffy
*Selected Poems*

George Eliot
*Middlemarch*
*The Mill on the Floss*

T.S. Eliot
*Selected Poems*
*The Waste Land*

F. Scott Fitzgerald
*The Great Gatsby*

E.M. Forster
*A Passage to India*

Brian Friel
*Translations*

Thomas Hardy
*Jude the Obscure*
*The Mayor of Casterbridge*
*The Return of the Native*
*Selected Poems*
*Tess of the d'Urbervilles*

Seamus Heaney
*Selected Poems from 'Opened Ground'*

Nathaniel Hawthorne
*The Scarlet Letter*

Homer
*The Iliad*
*The Odyssey*

Aldous Huxley
*Brave New World*

Kazuo Ishiguro
*The Remains of the Day*

Ben Jonson
*The Alchemist*

James Joyce
*Dubliners*

John Keats
*Selected Poems*

Philip Larkin
*The Whitsun Weddings and Selected Poems*

Christopher Marlowe
*Doctor Faustus*
*Edward II*

Arthur Miller
*Death of a Salesman*

John Milton
*Paradise Lost Books I & II*

Toni Morrison
*Beloved*

George Orwell
*Nineteen Eighty-Four*

Sylvia Plath
*Selected Poems*

Alexander Pope
*Rape of the Lock & Selected Poems*

William Shakespeare
*Antony and Cleopatra*
*As You Like It*
*Hamlet*
*Henry IV Part I*
*King Lear*
*Macbeth*
*Measure for Measure*
*The Merchant of Venice*
*A Midsummer Night's Dream*
*Much Ado About Nothing*
*Othello*
*Richard II*
*Richard III*
*Romeo and Juliet*
*The Taming of the Shrew*
*The Tempest*
*Twelfth Night*
*The Winter's Tale*

George Bernard Shaw
*Saint Joan*

Mary Shelley
*Frankenstein*

Jonathan Swift
*Gulliver's Travels and A Modest Proposal*

Alfred Tennyson
*Selected Poems*

Virgil
*The Aeneid*

Alice Walker
*The Color Purple*

Oscar Wilde
*The Importance of Being Earnest*

Tennessee Williams
*A Streetcar Named Desire*
*The Glass Menagerie*

Jeanette Winterson
*Oranges Are Not the Only Fruit*

John Webster
*The Duchess of Malfi*

Virginia Woolf
*To the Lighthouse*

William Wordsworth
*The Prelude and Selected Poems*

W.B. Yeats
*Selected Poems*

*Metaphysical Poets*